DISH IT UP

SIMON HOLST

good food ~ new food ~ fast food

NEW HOLLAND

First published in 2000 by New Holland Publishers (NZ) Ltd
Auckland • Sydney • London • Cape Town

218 Lake Road, Northcote, Auckland, New Zealand
14 Aquatic Drive, Frenchs Forest, NSW 2086, Australia
24 Nutford Place, London W1H 6DQ, United Kingdom
80 McKenzie Street, Cape Town 8001, South Africa

ISBN: 1-877246-42-5

Managing editor: Renée Lang
Cover and design: Christine Hansen
Typesetting: ArcherDesign
Editor: Amy Palmer
Photography: Lindsay Keats
Food styling: Simon and Alison Holst
Home economists: Simon Holst and Hilary Wilson-Hill
Props: Jania Bates

Colour reproduction by Colour Symphony Pte Ltd
Printed by Craft Print Pte Ltd, Singapore

Cover photograph: Fish Veracruz (see page 70)

Special thanks to **Theme** and **Freedom** of Wellington for providing the tableware used in the following photos:

Theme: Page 23, plate and bowl; page 24, striped plates and cutlery; page 27, square plate; page 41, rectangular plate; page 59, plate and bowl; page 61, plate and bowl; page 65, napkin; page 85, bamboo mat; page 93, plate and bowl; page 95, wine glasses and cutlery; page 101, casserole dish and plate; page 102, wine glasses.

Freedom: Page 6, bowl; page 15, striped plate; page 18, tray, bowl and plate; page 23, wicker tray; page 36, glass plate and tumblers; page 43, napkin and plate; page 48, silver bowl; page 53, plate, bowl and glasses; page 63, serving plate and placemat; page 73, bowl and tray; page 75, table runner; page 77, plates and bowl; page 83, sliver bowls and table runners; page 95, plates; page 102, plate; page 110, table runner; page 113, plate and napkin.

contents

Heartfelt thanks to everyone who has contributed to the production of this book – you know who you are. Extra special thanks of course to my wife, Sam, and children Isabella and Theo, for their support in general, and for putting up with me during the final stages of production... I think it was worth it in the end!

'One pan meals', made from scratch in a short space of time, was the original concept that I had in mind for this book. And while it certainly contains one-dish meals in the strictly literal sense it ended up being a somewhat broader concept. *Dish it Up* is all about the food that I cook at home – a style of cooking that I suspect is being adopted by many busy people. It usually comprises one main, almost stand-alone, dish that is served with simple accompaniments like rice, pasta or bread and perhaps a salad.

It's a style of cooking that reflects a shift away from the once traditional 'meat and three vegetables', which probably has a lot to do with the fact that these days people appear to have less time to spend in the kitchen. With two young children I know all about this, so I've come to rely on quick, effective ways to prepare and cook food.

The most popular piece of equipment in my kitchen is a large, deep frypan that gets used for almost every meal. If pasta or rice are to be part of the meal, then obviously they'll be cooked in a separate pot (or microwave bowl). Likewise a salad or side of simply cooked vegetables will involve an extra bowl or pot. But the main focus almost always emerges from that large frypan.

I've tried to include as wide a range of dishes in this book as possible so that most tastes are catered for. And now that all the hard work is done I hope you'll enjoy this eclectic collection as much as I've enjoyed putting it together.

Happy cooking!

Simon Holst

P.S. Throughout this book I have used either olive or canola oil for their potentially beneficial monounsaturated fatty acid content, but if you don't have them on hand – or would prefer to use other oils in their place, by all means do so. With a few exceptions, such as where I have used olive oil for its flavour, this will make little difference to the final product.

Curried chicken and kumara salad

This delicious salad is prepared in three different stages, but all of them are easy, and the result is worth the effort.

For 2–3 main course servings:
2 tablespoons plain unsweetened yoghurt
1 tablespoon sweet mango chutney
1 teaspoon curry powder
2 cloves garlic, chopped
300–400g boneless skinless chicken
500g kumara
1 cup (2–3 sticks) sliced celery
½ cup roasted cashews, peanuts or almonds, roughly chopped
¼ – ½ cup chopped dates
¼ cup chopped fresh coriander

Dressing
½ cup plain unsweetened yoghurt
1–2 tablespoons sweet mango chutney
3–4 tablespoons orange juice
1 teaspoon each curry powder and salt

Put the first measure of yoghurt, chutney and curry powder and the chopped garlic into a plastic bag. Add the chicken, then massage the bag so the chicken is evenly coated with the marinade. Set aside for at least 15 minutes (refrigerate for longer periods).

Peel the kumara and cut into 2–3cm cubes. Cook until tender either by microwaving on high (100%) in a covered container for 7–10 minutes or by boiling gently, then leave to cool to room temperature.

Cook the chicken by grilling 5–10cm from the heat, for 5–10 minutes on each side (depending on thickness) or until the outside has browned and the juices run clear when the chicken is pierced at the thickest part. Leave chicken to stand for 5–10 minutes, then cut into bite-sized pieces.

While the chicken cooks, stir the dressing ingredients together, thinning to the desired consistency with orange juice, and prepare the remaining salad ingredients.

Place the cooled well-drained kumara, the chicken and remaining ingredients (reserving a little of the coriander to garnish) in a large bowl, drizzle with dressing, then toss gently to combine.

Garnish with the reserved coriander and serve immediately or refrigerate until required.

Curried chicken and kumara salad

Smoked fish and cucumber salad with lemon-dill mayonnaise

I've made this salad with a number of different types of fish, ranging from hot-smoked salmon to smoked kahawai, depending on what has been available or how I've been feeling, and it has been delicious with all of them. Dress it up or down as it suits you.

The recipe below actually makes more of the mayonnaise than you require to make the salad, but the extra keeps well in the fridge for 1–2 weeks and is so good I'm sure you'll find plenty of other uses for it anyway...

Lemon Mayonnaise
1 medium egg
finely grated rind of ½ lemon
2 tablespoons lemon juice
1 teaspoon Dijon mustard
1 clove garlic, peeled
½ teaspoon salt
black pepper
½ –1 cup canola or light olive oil

For 2–3 large servings:
Salad
250–350g hot-smoked fish
½ telegraph cucumber, quartered lengthwise and sliced
1 cup (2–3 sticks) sliced celery
1 medium yellow or red capsicum, deseeded
     and cubed
2 spring onions, sliced

Dressing
½ cup Lemon Mayonnaise (see above or see note)
2 tablespoons lemon juice
1–2 tablespoons chopped fresh dill
     (or 1 teaspoon dried)
salt and pepper to taste

To make the mayonnaise, put the egg, lemon rind and juice, mustard, garlic, salt and a grind of black pepper into a food processor or blender and process until well combined. With the machine running at medium-fast start adding the oil in a thin stream. Add enough oil to form a thick creamy mixture that holds its shape when the blender/processor is stopped.

Transfer the mayonnaise to an airtight container and refrigerate until required.

To assemble the salad, break the fish into bite-sized pieces or flakes, carefully removing any bones and skin, then place in a large bowl. Add the prepared vegetables to the bowl, reserving some of the sliced spring onion greens to garnish.

Measure the mayonnaise into a small bowl or cup, add the lemon juice and dill, then stir until mixed. Season to taste with salt and pepper.

Add the dressing to the salad and toss gently to combine. Garnish with the reserved spring onion and serve immediately or refrigerate until required. This salad makes a great meal accompanied with crusty bread or steamed rice.

Note:
If you don't want to make your own mayonnaise, use an American-style mayonnaise, adding the finely grated rind of ½ a lemon.

Gado gado salad (vegetables with peanut sauce)

I'm a sucker for almost anything served with a peanut sauce – I guess this helps explain why I find this simple yet substantial salad so delicious.

Assemble a platter of vegetables, top with the sauce and wait for the compliments!

For 3–4 servings:
Peanut Sauce (makes about 1½ cups)
½ teaspoon tamarind paste (or 1–2 tablespoons lemon juice)
1 cup boiling water
100g roasted peanuts
1 clove garlic
1–2 teaspoons grated ginger
1 teaspoon minced chilli (or 1 small red chilli)
1 tablespoon each brown sugar and dark soy sauce

Vegetable Platter
lettuce leaves or spinach, washed with stalks removed
a selection of 3 (or more) of:
    cooked potatoes, sliced
    green beans (or snake beans), lightly cooked
    cucumber, halved lengthwise, deseeded and sliced
    tofu, cubed or sliced
    bean sprouts
    hard-boiled eggs, quartered or sliced
    chopped fresh basil or coriander (optional)

To make the sauce, measure the tamarind paste into a small bowl, then add the boiling water. Break up the tamarind and leave to stand for 2–3 minutes.

Place the remaining sauce ingredients into a food processor or blender. Process briefly then strain in the tamarind water (or lemon juice and water), discarding the tamarind pulp.

Process again to make a fairly smooth paste. Transfer the sauce to a microwave bowl or pot and boil for 2–3 minutes, or until the sauce has thickened to desired consistency. Set aside to cool (a little) while preparing the vegetables.

To assemble the salad, cover a platter (or individual plates) with a layer of lettuce or spinach leaves. Add a layer of sliced potatoes, then any of your other selected foods, finishing with the bean sprouts or eggs. Cover generously with the peanut sauce, garnish with some chopped fresh basil or coriander, and serve.

Pasta and tuna salad

Pasta and tuna are another great salad pairing. In this salad I've teamed them up with ingredients of the 'classic' Salad Niçoise. Obviously the Niçoise combination of tuna, olives, eggs and capers works well but I think they all go really well with pasta too.

For 3–4 servings:
250g small pasta shells
2 eggs
150g fresh green beans, topped and tailed
3 ripe tomatoes, cubed
12–16 black olives
1–2 tablespoons capers
½ cup mayonnaise
2 tablespoons each lemon juice and olive oil
½ teaspoon salt
black pepper
210g can tuna (in oil or brine), drained and flaked
¼ cup chopped fresh parsley

Put the pasta on to cook in plenty of boiling water, and add the eggs to hard boil.

Boil or steam the green beans until tender (I cook these in a sieve over the pasta water). When cooked, drain and cut into 4–5cm lengths. Place the cooked beans, tomatoes, olives and capers in a bowl. Toss these together then add the mayonnaise, lemon juice, oil, salt and pepper. Mix again until well combined. Add the tuna to the vegetable mixture.

Drain the cooked pasta, remove and peel the eggs. Add the tuna mixture and the chopped parsley to the pasta. Stir gently to combine. Transfer to a serving bowl (or bowls) and garnish with the quartered or roughly chopped hard-boiled eggs.

I will happily eat this salad as a meal accompanied with some crusty bread, but of course it can also be served (warm or chilled) as a starter or side dish.

Californian pasta salad

This is my version of a salad I tried in San Francisco. It was (justifiably, I think) the most popular salad served in the Macy's food hall. The original version was made with prawns, but I actually think surimi works just as well or you can use a mixture of both.

When you are out shopping for the ingredients, make sure you look for marinated artichoke hearts (usually packed in oil with some other seasonings). These are much more interesting than their brine-packed cousins!

For 3–4 servings:

200g large pasta shells or other shapes
1 small head broccoli, cut into bite-sized florets
300–400g can or jar marinated artichoke hearts
250g cooked peeled prawns or surimi
2 spring onions, finely sliced
chopped fresh dill to garnish

Dressing

½ cup plain unsweetened yoghurt
½ cup lite sour cream
2 tablespoons lemon (or lime) juice
2 tablespoons chopped fresh dill
½ –1 teaspoon salt
black pepper to taste

Cook the pasta in plenty of boiling water. Cook the broccoli in a little water (or over the pasta) until just tender, then rinse with plenty of cold water.

Measure dressing ingredients into a small bowl and mix, adding salt and pepper to taste.

Drain the artichoke hearts, and cut into halves or quarters. Drain the cooked pasta (slightly underdone is best) and rinse under cold water to cool it quickly. Combine the pasta, broccoli, and half the artichoke pieces and prawns (or surimi) in a large bowl. Add the dressing and the chopped spring onions, then stir gently until well combined. Arrange remaining artichoke hearts and prawns or surimi on top then garnish with the chopped dill. Refrigerate until required if you are making it in advance.

Serve alone, with crusty bread or as part of a buffet.

Asian-style beef salad

This dish is inspired by Thai beef salads, although once again the ethnic boundaries have become a little blurred. It is delicious served alone, or for a more substantial meal, serve it with a bowl of steamed fragrant rice.

For 2–3 servings:

Dressing/Marinade

2 tablespoons each sweet chilli sauce and Kikkoman soy sauce
1 tablespoon each wine vinegar and sesame oil
300–450g thickly sliced (2–3cm) fillet steak
2 tablespoons lime juice
1–2 teaspoons oil (to cook)

Salad

¼ – ½ telegraph cucumber, halved lengthwise and sliced
1 red, orange or yellow capsicum, deseeded and cubed
1–2 spring onions, finely sliced
about 3 cups mesclun or mixed salad greens
¼ cup each chopped fresh mint and coriander
1 avocado, diced

Measure the first 4 dressing ingredients into a screw-top jar and shake to combine. Place the beef in an unpunctured plastic bag, then add half the dressing/marinade mixture. Massage the bag so the beef is covered with the marinade, then set aside for 30 minutes or longer (refrigerate overnight if desired).

Add the lime juice to the remaining dressing, shake to combine then set aside.

Toss the prepared vegetables together with the spring onions, mesclun (or salad greens), mint and coriander in a large bowl.

Heat a large pan over a high heat, then add a little (about 1 teaspoon) oil. Cook the steak for 2–3 minutes per side so both sides are well browned. (You may need to vary the cooking time depending on the thickness of the steak and how rare you want it.) Remove steak from the pan and allow to rest for about 5 minutes, before cutting into 5mm slices.

While the steak rests, peel and dice the avocado, then toss it with the other vegetables and half of the remaining dressing. Arrange the salad greens on individual plates or a platter. Fan the sliced meat over the greens then drizzle with the remaining dressing.

Serve immediately, as is or accompanied with some steamed fragrant rice.

Asian-style beef salad

Seared scallop and asparagus salad

This salad must be prepared in several different stages, then assembled just before serving, but the results are definitely worth a little time and effort!

I love the crispy rice noodles and always find cooking them a little like magic, but if you don't have any on hand – or just can't be bothered cooking them – they can be omitted.

For 2–3 servings:
24 scallops
1 tablespoon each sweet chilli sauce and Kikkoman soy sauce
1 teaspoon sesame oil
50–75g rice vermicelli
canola oil (to fry)
2–3 cups mixed salad vegetables (young lettuce leaves, mesclun, sliced cucumber, sliced red/orange/yellow capsicums, halved cherry tomatoes etc.)
1 bunch (200–250g) asparagus
1 tablespoon canola oil
about ¼ cup chopped fresh coriander

Dressing
2 tablespoons each sweet chilli sauce, fish sauce and rice (or wine) vinegar
1 tablespoon oyster sauce
2 teaspoons sesame oil
1 tablespoon grated ginger
1 clove garlic, minced
2–4 tablespoons water

Mix the scallops with the first measure of sweet chilli sauce, soy sauce and sesame oil, then leave to stand while you prepare the remaining ingredients.

To make the dressing, measure the first seven ingredients and 2 tablespoons of the water into a medium-sized screw-top jar or blender and shake or blend until well combined. Taste and add the remaining water (and shake or blend again) if you think it is too salty.

Separate the vermicelli into two or three smaller bundles. Heat 1–2cm of oil in a large pan or wok until it is hot enough that one or two strands of vermicelli puff up more or less instantly when dropped in. When the oil is hot enough carefully drop in one of the bundles. When the first side has puffed up and turned slightly off-white turn the 'nest' over using a fish slice or tongs, and puff the other side. Remove the cooked vermicelli from the pan and drain on paper towels. Repeat with the remaining bundle/s.

Place the prepared salad vegetables in a large bowl or plastic bag.

When you have everything else ready, slice the asparagus diagonally, into 5–6cm pieces, and heat the second measure of oil in a large non-stick pan. Add the asparagus and stir-fry until it is just tender, then add the scallops with their marinade. Cook, stirring frequently, for 1–2 minutes longer until the scallops are just cooked, then remove from the heat.

Pour about half the dressing and half of the coriander into the salad vegetables and toss until evenly mixed. Arrange the greens on individual plates or a serving platter, then arrange the nests of vermicelli over them. Pile the scallops and asparagus on top of the vermicelli and sprinkle with the remaining coriander.

Drizzle over a little extra dressing and serve immediately. Don't worry if you have dressing left over – it keeps well in the fridge and can be used in other salads, or even over warm or cold meats, chicken or fish.

Seared scallop and asparagus salad

Couscous and chickpea salad with orange-balsamic dressing

Couscous is a wonderful food for summer – all it needs is a quick soak in boiling water and it's ready to go. Use it in place of rice or pasta as a side dish or accompaniment, or with a few embellishments it can form the basis of a meal. The orange-balsamic dressing and currants used here give the salad an interesting, slightly sweet flavour.

While this salad is substantial enough to serve as a vegetarian main as is, it is also good with some cooked lamb or chicken added. Simply brush one or two lamb loins or boneless skinless chicken breasts with the dressing and grill until cooked then slice and toss into, or serve on top of, the salad.

For 2–3 large servings:

1 cup couscous
¼ cup currants
1 teaspoon instant vegetable or chicken stock powder (optional)
1¼ cups boiling water
300g can chickpeas, rinsed and drained
1 red capsicum, deseeded and cubed
2 spring onions, finely sliced
½ cup Kalamata olives
2–3 tablespoons chopped fresh herbs (try a mixture of parsley, coriander and mint)

Dressing

¼ cup orange juice
2 tablespoons each balsamic vinegar and extra virgin olive oil
2 teaspoons ground cumin
½ teaspoon salt
1 clove garlic, peeled and finely chopped

Measure the couscous, currants and instant stock (if using) into a large bowl. Add the boiling water, then cover and leave to stand for about 5 minutes while you prepare the remaining ingredients. Fluff the soaked couscous with a fork, then add the chickpeas, diced capsicum, spring onions, olives (don't forget to warn diners if using unpitted olives) and most of the chopped herbs to the bowl.

Prepare the dressing by adding all the ingredients to a screw-top jar, then shaking to combine. Pour the dressing over the salad and toss to combine. Garnish with the remaining chopped herbs and serve.

Ham and pasta salad with lemon-mustard dressing

Although they are always popular, ham and pasta salads are hardly a new idea – but the dressing gives this version a real lift!

This delicious salad is well capable of standing alone and forming the basis of an easy meal on its own, but also makes a great addition to a barbecue buffet.

For 4 large servings:

250g large pasta shapes (bows, ruote/wagon wheels, shells etc.)
150–200g sliced ham, cut into narrow strips
1 cup (2–3 medium sticks) sliced celery
2 firm ripe tomatoes, quartered and sliced
½–1 small red onion, diced
1–2 tablespoons chopped fresh chives or parsley to garnish

Dressing

½ cup mayonnaise
finely grated rind 1 lemon
¼ cup lemon juice
2 tablespoons olive (or canola) oil
1 tablespoon wholegrain (or Dijon) mustard
½ teaspoon salt
black pepper to taste

Cook the pasta in plenty of lightly salted boiling water. As soon as it is cooked, drain then cool the pasta by rinsing it in plenty of cold water. (Overcooking the pasta will result in a soggy, unpleasant salad.)

Prepare the dressing by whisking the first six dressing ingredients together in a large bowl, then adding black pepper to taste. Add the cooled drained pasta, ham and prepared vegetables to the dressing and stir gently to combine.

Garnish with the chopped herbs and serve immediately, or store in the fridge until required (salad can be prepared several hours in advance if desired).

Variation:

Try using ¼ cup each of lite sour cream and plain unsweetened yoghurt in place of the mayonnaise if you like.

Ham and pasta salad with lemon-mustard dressing

Sushi rice salad

If you like sushi, you'll love this delicious salad. It contains all of my favourite sushi ingredients, but is even easier to prepare than sushi, because instead of being neatly rolled up, they are just tossed together! If you have favourite ingredients that are not here, why not try adding them to your own 'customised' version?

The rice and dressing may be prepared in advance, but the salad itself is best assembled shortly before serving.

For 2–3 main course servings:

1 cup medium-grain rice
2 cups boiling water
50–100g cold-smoked salmon (or 100–200g surimi)
pickled (pink) ginger, thinly sliced (optional)
2–3 sheets yaki nori (grilled seaweed sheets)
1 avocado, peeled and cubed
½ telegraph cucumber, cubed
1 medium carrot, finely diced

Dressing

2 tablespoons each sherry and canola oil
1 tablespoon each Kikkoman soy sauce, rice (or wine)
    vinegar and sugar
½ teaspoon salt
1–2 teaspoons wasabi paste to taste
1–2 teaspoons grated fresh ginger (optional)

Cover rice with the boiling water, then cover and microwave at 50% power for 15 minutes so the grains are completely tender. While the rice cooks, prepare the dressing by measuring all the ingredients into a screw-top jar then shaking until well blended.

When the rice is cooked, pour in half the dressing and stir until well combined. Leave the rice to stand until cool (refrigerate if preparing in advance).

Cut the salmon into strips about 1cm wide (or shred the surimi), and cut or tear the nori sheets into strips about 1cm wide and 4cm long.

Stir the avocado, cucumber and carrot into the rice along with the salmon (or surimi), pickled ginger, nori (reserve a little to garnish) and the remaining dressing. Toss to combine. Garnish with the reserved nori strips and serve. Accompany with little bowls of extra soy sauce and wasabi if desired.

Variation:

The soy sauce in the dressing gives the salad a good flavour, but does 'muddy' the colour a little. If you prefer, omit it from the dressing and serve on the side in little dipping sauce bowls.

Peanutty noodle salad

I'm quite happy to eat a large bowl of a salad like this on its own as a main course, although if you are going to serve it as a main you may want to add some warm or cold shredded chicken. You can use leftover home-cooked chicken, or for a really easy alternative, pick up a pre-cooked chicken at the supermarket.

For 4 servings:

Dressing

¼ cup peanut butter
2 teaspoons sesame oil
1 tablespoon rice (or wine) vinegar
2 tablespoons Kikkoman soy sauce
2 tablespoons sweet chilli sauce
1 clove garlic, minced
1–2 tablespoons grated fresh ginger
¼ cup hot water
2–3 tablespoons chopped coriander
salt to taste

Salad

250g fine egg noodles
1 large carrot, cut into fine strips
½ cup whole green beans
½ telegraph cucumber, halved lengthwise, deseeded
    and cut into fine strips
1–2 cups shredded cabbage
1–2 spring onions, cut lengthwise into fine strips
300–400g cooked shredded chicken (optional)
2 tablespoons lime (or lemon) juice
sliced spring onion greens or coriander to garnish

Combine all the dressing ingredients, except for the coriander and salt, in a blender or screw-top jar and blend or shake until well combined. Add the coriander and salt to taste. Leave the dressing to stand while you prepare the remaining ingredients.

Bring a large pot of water to the boil then add the noodles. Cook the noodles until they are just done (over-done noodles will be soggy and weak), then drain them and toss with a little vegetable oil. Set aside to cool.

Combine the carrot and beans in a shallow pan, cover with hot water and boil for about 1 minute. Drain and set aside with the noodles. Add the cucumber, the shredded cabbage and the white part of the spring onions to the other vegetables, reserving the spring onion greens to garnish.

Thin the dressing with 1–2 tablespoons of extra water if you think it looks too thick, then toss the noodles, vegetables, shredded chicken (if using) and dressing together in a large bowl. If possible leave to stand for 15–30 minutes then drizzle with the lime or lemon juice and toss again. Garnish with sliced spring onion greens and/or coriander before serving.

Two-minute noodle salad with a Thai twist

Two minute noodles make a great (if unusual sounding) addition to salads – they are actually cooked before they are dried so they can be crumbled and added to salads as they are. I've added an interesting Thai-inspired dressing to this salad to give it an extra lift.

For 2–3 servings:
200–250g chicken tenderloins
1 teaspoon each Kikkoman soy sauce and sesame oil
1–2 teaspoons canola oil (to cook)

Dressing
1 clove garlic
2 teaspoons finely chopped lemon grass
1 teaspoon red curry paste
2 teaspoons sugar
2 tablespoons each fish sauce and rice vinegar
¼ cup coconut cream

Salad
¼ medium cabbage, shredded
1 large carrot, cut into fine strips
3–4 tablespoons chopped coriander
½ cup roasted peanuts
1 (85g) packet two minute noodles

Place the tenderloins in a plastic bag and add the soy sauce and sesame oil. Massage the bag so the chicken is evenly coated with the marinade, then close bag and leave to stand for at least 5 minutes.

To make the dressing, measure the fist six dressing ingredients into a blender or food processor and blend until smooth and well combined. Add the coconut cream and process again. Leave to stand while you prepare the salad.

Combine the cabbage and carrot in a large bowl with the chopped coriander and the peanuts.

Heat 1–2 teaspoons oil in a frypan and cook the chicken over a high heat for 2–3 minutes per side, or until it is no longer pink in the middle. Remove the chicken from the pan and leave to stand for about 5 minutes.

Crush the cake of noodles just enough so there are no large clumps, then toss the noodles through the vegetable mixture with about two thirds of the dressing. Add remaining dressing if you think the salad looks too dry.

Slice the cooked chicken and toss this through the salad, or divide the salad between individual plates, then top with the whole or sliced chicken tenderloins.

Note:
This makes a delicious side salad (for 4–6 people) with the chicken left out.

Tom yum plus

Tom yum or shrimp (prawn) soup is often regarded as one of the trade-mark Thai dishes. While different versions of the same soup vary in complexity, the one thing they have in common is the hot and sour base.

The base for this version is simple to prepare, but as well as the prawns I have added some additional vegetables and rice noodles to make it a little more substantial.

For 2–3 servings:
250g (about 12) whole uncooked prawns
4 cups water
2cm fresh ginger, finely chopped
1 stalk lemon grass, halved lengthwise
3–4 kaffir lime leaves*
½ –1 teaspoon minced red chilli to taste
1 stalk lemon grass, very finely sliced
3–4 tablespoons lime juice
50–100g rice noodles
250g button mushrooms
1 medium carrot, cut into fine matchsticks
250g firm fish, cubed
2–3 tablespoons fish sauce to taste
2 tablespoons chopped fresh coriander
1 spring onion, sliced
sliced red chilli and additional coriander to garnish

Start by preparing the basic stock. Remove the tails from the prawns and set aside. Place the heads in a large pot with the water, ginger, first stalk of lemon grass and lime leaves. Bring to the boil and simmer for about 10 minutes. While the stock simmers, peel and devein the prawn tails (add the shells to the stock if you like).

Strain the stock into a clean pot (I usually save the lime leaves and return them to the stock) then add the next six ingredients. Add ½ teaspoon of the minced chilli first, then taste and add more only if you think it is required. Simmer gently for about 3 minutes until the noodles and vegetables are cooked, then add the prawn tails and cubed fish. Simmer for 1–2 minutes longer, or until the fish has turned white and is just cooked through. Remove from the heat, then add fish sauce to taste and the chopped coriander and spring onion.

Divide soup between serving bowls and garnish with some thinly sliced red chilli and a few coriander leaves and serve immediately.

*Kaffir lime leaves are available fresh or dried from stores specialising in Asian foods. Buy fresh leaves if you can as they have the best flavour and scent, but dried ones will do if you can't get fresh. If you can't find lime leaves, use fresh lemon leaves instead – these have a reasonable flavour although not as scented as kaffir lime.

Tom yum plus

Vegetable and bean soup

This colourful soup definitely contains everything required to constitute a meal in its own right! Although it can be served as something warm and comforting in winter, it is somehow also light enough to be served in summer too.

The list of ingredients looks long, but like most soups it is actually remarkably simple to prepare. Several of the ingredients listed below are 'optional' but I think they all add something, so if you've got them on hand, why not add them?

For 6–8 servings:

2 tablespoons olive oil
1–2 rashers bacon, chopped (optional)
1 large onion, finely diced
2 cloves garlic, peeled and chopped
2 small dried chillies, chopped (optional)
2 medium carrots, finely diced
2 medium sticks celery, thinly sliced
1 medium potato, cubed
4 cups chicken or vegetable stock
425g can kidney beans, drained and rinsed
440g can four-bean mix, drained and rinsed
425g can Italian seasoned tomatoes
¾ cup small pasta shapes
1 cup frozen peas
2 cups finely sliced cabbage (optional)
3–4 tablespoons chopped fresh parsley
2 tablespoons pesto or ¼ cup chopped fresh basil
　　(optional)
salt and pepper to taste
grated parmesan cheese and pesto to garnish

Heat the oil in a large pot over a medium heat. Cook the bacon (if using) until golden then add the onion, garlic and chillies. Cook, stirring occasionally, for 5 minutes or until the onion is soft and clear.

Stir in the carrots, celery and potato and cook for 1–2 minutes longer. Add the stock, beans and tomatoes and bring the soup to the boil, then reduce the heat and simmer for 30 minutes or until the potato is tender.

Add the pasta, peas, cabbage and herbs. Simmer for 10–15 minutes or until the pasta is tender but still firm. Add some water if you think the soup is too thick, then season to taste with salt and pepper.

Ladle into warm soup bowls, topping each serving with a little freshly grated parmesan cheese and a spoonful of pesto.

Note:

For vegetarian soup, omit the bacon and use vegetable rather than chicken stock.

Red bean and rice soup

I started making this delicious soup with red kidney beans instead of the black beans I used to use because the little black beans required seem to be getting harder and harder to find! I think the red beans work remarkably well, the only real difference is that the soup lacks the dramatic colour the black beans used to give.

For 6–8 servings:

3 tablespoons olive (or canola) oil
2 medium-large onions, diced
3 large cloves garlic, finely chopped
1 teaspoon minced red chilli
1 tablespoon cumin
1 teaspoon oregano
3 cups chicken or vegetable stock
1 cup long-grain brown rice
2 x 425g cans red kidney beans, drained and rinsed
½–1 cup water (if required)
salt and pepper to taste
sour cream, croutons, chopped coriander to garnish

Heat the oil in a large pot, add the onions and garlic and cook, stirring occasionally, for about 5 minutes or until the onions are soft and turning clear.

Stir in the chilli, cumin and oregano and cook for 1–2 minutes longer, then add the stock and the rice. Bring to the boil then reduce the heat to a gentle simmer. Cover with a tight fitting lid and cook for 30 minutes.

Stir the beans into the pot along with enough extra water (if required) to ensure everything is covered. Replace the lid and cook for 15–20 minutes longer, or until the rice is very tender (stir occasionally and add a little extra water if it looks too dry).

Tip about half the soup into a blender or food processor and process until fairly smooth (you may have to do this in two batches). Stir the purée back into the rest of the soup, then thin with milk or water if desired and season to taste with salt and pepper.

Serve as is or garnish with a spoonful of sour cream, a handful of croutons and a little chopped coriander.

Note:

If you can find canned black beans by all means use them! If you want to use dried beans (red or black) soak 1½ cups dried beans overnight, then change the water and boil until very tender. (Remember kidney beans must be boiled vigorously for at least 10 minutes during cooking.)

Curry laksa

I love laksa, and tend to indulge my passion whenever visiting markets or food-halls! I think a large bowl of laksa makes a great meal, especially when accompanied with bread like roti.

Some purists insist that authentic laksa must be made using rice noodles, but my favourite market versions are often made with fresh egg noodles instead, and so these are what I tend to use at home too.

For 4 servings:
2–3 teaspoons curry powder
2–3 tablespoons cashew nuts
1 tablespoon chopped fresh ginger
2 cloves garlic
2–3 tablespoons chopped fresh lemon grass
finely chopped rind of 1 lime
1–2 teaspoons green or red curry paste (optional)
2 tablespoons canola oil
400ml can coconut cream
3 cups chicken stock (or 3 cups water plus 3 teaspoons
    instant chicken stock)
2 tablespoons light soy sauce
500g fresh egg noodles
200g fried tofu
about 100g bean sprouts
250g fish balls
250g raw peeled prawns (or cooked chicken meat)
2 hard boiled eggs (optional)
chopped fresh coriander and/or spring onion to garnish

Combine the first eight ingredients in a blender or food processor (or mortar and pestle) and process to make a smooth paste. The Thai curry paste is not absolutely necessary, but I think it adds to the 'depth' of flavour. Transfer the paste to a large pot and cook, stirring continuously for 1 minute.

Add the coconut cream, stock and soy sauce then simmer for about 10 minutes. During this time, divide the noodles, tofu and bean sprouts between individual serving bowls.

Bring the soup to the boil and add the fish balls and peeled prawns or chicken meat, and cook for 1–2 minutes. Ladle the soup into the bowls, dividing the fish balls and prawns (or chicken) evenly between each.

Garnish with a few extra bean sprouts, quartered or chopped hard-boiled egg (if using), some chopped coriander and/or sliced spring onion and serve immediately.

Variation:
One major advantage of using rice noodles is they keep almost indefinitely in the pantry. If you want to use them in place of egg noodles, soak 250g thick rice sticks for 5 minutes in boiling water, then proceed as above.

Fish chowder

Fish chowder makes an excellent easy meal at any time of the year – it is light enough to be enjoyed during summer, but is also warm and comforting on a cold winter's evening.

For 3–4 servings:
1 tablespoon olive oil
25g butter
1 medium onion, diced
100g bacon, cut into 1cm squares
2 sticks celery, thinly sliced
2 medium potatoes, cut into 1cm cubes
1 medium carrot, finely diced
2½ cups milk
½ teaspoon garlic salt
500g fish fillets, cubed
1 tablespoon chopped fresh dill (optional)
1 tablespoon cornflour
salt and pepper to taste
chopped fresh dill or parsley to garnish

Heat the oil and butter together in a large pot, then add the diced onion and cook until the onion softens. Add the bacon, celery, potatoes and carrot to the pot and cook, stirring frequently to prevent browning, for about 5 minutes.

Add 2 cups of milk and the garlic salt and simmer for about 10 minutes or until the potato is just tender, then add the cubed fish and dill (if using). Mix the remaining milk with the cornflour and add this to the pot. Bring the chowder to the boil, then reduce the heat and simmer for 5 minutes.

Season to taste with salt and pepper, then ladle into large bowls, garnish with chopped dill or parsley and serve accompanied with crusty garlic bread.

Curried pumpkin and kumara soup

Pumpkin soup was one of the fall-back meals from my student days – pumpkins were used as a 'loss leader' by the supermarkets, and at as little as one cent each they were definitely popular student fare!

Pumpkin soup served with a chunk of crusty bread still makes a great easy meal. This version is given a slight twist with the addition of a hint of Thai red curry paste and some coconut cream to make it especially smooth.

For 6–8 servings:
2 tablespoons olive (or canola) oil
2 medium onions, diced
1–2 tablespoons red curry paste*
1kg peeled and seeded pumpkin (or butternut squash)
500g kumara, peeled
3 cups hot water
3 teaspoons instant chicken or vegetable stock
1 cup coconut cream
½–1 teaspoon salt

Heat the oil in a very large pot, then add the roughly diced onions and cook, stirring occasionally, until the onions have softened, then add the curry paste (or powder) and cook for 1–2 minutes longer, stirring frequently.

While the onion cooks, cut the pumpkin (or squash) and kumara into chunks 2–3cm thick. When the curry paste is cooked, add these to the pan along with the water and stock.

Stir to combine, then cover the pot with a close-fitting lid and simmer for 25–30 minutes or until the pumpkin and kumara are very soft.

Working in batches transfer the soup mixture to a blender or food processor and process until very smooth. Return the processed soup to the pot, then add the coconut cream and salt to taste.

Serve immediately garnished with a swirl of additional coconut (or regular) cream, or reheat when required. Leftovers freeze well.

*Vary the quantity to taste (you can also replace this with curry powder if you like).

Spicy cheese and salsa chowder

I know this soup sounds unusual, but it really does taste great! I like it to be noticeably hot, so I include a little chilli powder and use a 'medium' salsa, but if you want a milder version simply omit the chilli and opt for a mild salsa.

Of course this substantial soup will stand up by itself, but if you want to make it extra memorable, serve it topped with a little of one or more of the optional extras listed below. Alternatively serve ungarnished but accompany with a selection of the toppings, so your diners can add their own.

For 4–6 servings:
1 tablespoon olive (or canola) oil
1 medium-large onion, diced
¼ teaspoon chilli powder (optional)
½ teaspoon each cumin and oregano
2 cups hot water
500g potatoes, peeled and diced
2 teaspoons instant chicken or vegetable stock
410g can cream-style corn
1 cup milk
300g jar (about 1¼ cups) salsa, mild or medium
1–1½ cups grated tasty cheese
salt and pepper to taste

Heat the oil in a large pot, then add the onion and cook until softened. Stir in the chilli powder, cumin and oregano and cook for about a minute longer.

Add the hot water, potatoes and instant stock then cover and simmer for about 10 minutes, or until the potatoes are very tender. Working in batches, transfer the mixture to a blender or food processor, and process until smooth.

Return the purée to the pot and add the corn, milk and salsa. Stir to combine then simmer for about 5 minutes. Remove from the heat and stir in the grated cheese. Taste and season with salt and pepper if required.

Serve as is or topped or accompanied with bowls of one or more of the following optional extras:

sour cream (or plain unsweetened yoghurt)
chopped coriander
sliced or diced avocado
diced tomato
croutons or crushed corn chips
finely diced red or green capsicum

Spicy cheese and salsa chowder

Salmon and rice packages

These easy salmon packages look and taste great but are really very easy to make. This is a great combination which I think makes them perfect for entertaining.

For 4 servings:

500–600g salmon fillet/s
2 tablespoons each Kikkoman soy sauce and lemon (or lime) juice
1 teaspoon sesame oil
2 teaspoons wasabi paste
2 cups cooked rice
1 medium red capsicum, deseeded and finely diced
1 medium carrot, finely diced
1–2 sticks celery, finely diced
1 spring onion, thinly sliced
1 teaspoon celery salt
½ teaspoon garlic salt
8–12 sheets filo pastry
1–2 tablespoons olive oil or melted butter

Lie the salmon fillet/s skin side down on a board. Hold the thin (tail) end and, with sharp knife, cut through the flesh to the skin. Keeping the knife parallel to the board run the knife along the inside surface of the skin to remove it from the flesh (keeping tension on the skin by pulling the tail end with your free hand makes this easier). Discard the skin and cut the fillet/s into four equal portions.

Turn the oven on to preheat to 200°C. Measure the soy sauce, lemon (or lime) juice, sesame oil and wasabi paste into a plastic bag and mix together. Add the fish and massage the bag so the pieces are evenly coated with the marinade. Leave to stand while you prepare the remaining ingredients.

Place the rice, finely diced vegetables, sliced spring onion, and celery and garlic salts in a large bowl and mix thoroughly.

Lay the first sheet of filo pastry out on a clean dry surface, brush lightly with oil, then cover with another sheet of filo (oil this and add another layer of filo if you like). Place ½ – ¾ cup of the rice filling in the middle of one end, then top with a piece of the salmon. Fold the edges of the filo in, then roll up to form a neat package. Place package salmon side up, on a lightly oiled or baking paper lined baking tray or sponge-roll tin. Repeat the layering-rolling process to make four parcels.

Place parcels in the oven and bake for 15–20 minutes until the filo is golden brown.

Arrange cooked parcels on plates and serve accompanied with a crisp green salad.

Easy East-West pork pie

This easy pie has a delicious Asian-influenced pork filling, enclosed in a crisp pastry crust. As the pie is rather thin and flat, the filling does not need to be pre-cooked, which makes the whole thing very easy to prepare, especially when you use pre-rolled pastry.

For 4 servings:
2 square sheets pre-rolled flaky pastry (about 300g)
1 large clove garlic
4 spring onions, sliced
500g minced pork
1 medium apple, grated
2 tablespoons sweet chilli sauce
1 tablespoon Kikkoman soy sauce
1 teaspoon sesame oil
½ teaspoon salt
½ cup dry breadcrumbs
lightly beaten egg (or milk or water) to glaze

Place the pastry sheets on the bench to thaw and preheat the oven to 200°C while you prepare the filling mixture.

Place the peeled garlic, sliced spring onions, pork and grated apple in a food processor fitted with a metal chopping blade and process until well mixed. Add the chilli sauce, soy sauce and sesame oil then process again. Sprinkle the salt and breadcrumbs over the mixture then process in short bursts until evenly mixed.

Place the pastry sheets on a lightly floured bench and gently roll them out to about 30cm square. Lay the first sheet on a baking paper lined oven tray or baking sheet, then spread the filling out over the surface leaving a 3cm gap around the edges. Brush the exposed pastry edge with water, then lay the second sheet over the filling. Gently press the edges together to seal, then fold the sealed edges under and flute the edge with your fingers or the tines of a fork. Using a fork or sharp knife make air vents every few centimetres over the surface.

Brush the pie with a little lightly beaten egg (or milk or water) then bake at 200°C for 20 minutes, then reduce the heat to 180°C and bake for a further 20 minutes.

Cut into squares and serve warm or cool. A little extra sweet chilli sauce makes an ideal accompaniment.

Mushroom and potato pie

Adding a pastry top turns this simple casserole into a delicious and impressive looking 'single crust' pie.

For 4 servings:
500g (3–4 medium) waxy potatoes
2 tablespoons olive (or canola) oil
1 medium onion, peeled, quartered and sliced
1 clove garlic, peeled and chopped
200g mushrooms, sliced (use opened brown caps for maximum flavour)
½ teaspoon basil (or 1 tablespoon basil pesto)
¼ teaspoon thyme
½ teaspoon salt
black pepper to taste
1 cup (250g) sour cream
½ teaspoon salt
black pepper
1–2 sheets pre-rolled flaky pastry
milk or lightly beaten egg to glaze

Scrub the potatoes, then cut them into 5mm slices. Place them in an oven bag or covered microwave dish and cook on high power for 10 minutes, stirring gently after 5 minutes. (Alternatively, boil the potato slices until just tender, handling them gently to avoid breaking them up.)

Heat the oil in a large pan, add the onion and garlic and sauté until the onion is soft and turning clear. Stir in the mushrooms, herbs and salt and pepper. Cook, stirring frequently, until the mushrooms have wilted.

Turn the oven on to preheat to 220°C. While the oven heats, non-stick spray or lightly oil a 20 x 25cm (or round) casserole or deep pie dish. Arrange half of the potato slices evenly over the bottom of the dish, then cover this with the mushroom mixture and then the remaining potato slices. Stir together the sour cream and the second measures of salt and pepper then pour this evenly over the layered potatoes and mushrooms.

Roll out the pastry (if necessary), until it will cover the casserole/pie dish. Brush the edge of the dish with a little water, then lay the pastry over the filling mixture. Gently press around the edge of the dish and trim off any excess. Decorate the edge by patterning it with the tines of a fork (or fluting with your fingers) and puncture the pastry at 5cm intervals over the surface. Brush with a little milk or beaten egg to glaze, then bake at 220°C for about 15 minutes until the pastry is golden brown.

Serve with a salad or cooked vegetables and some crusty bread.

Easy East-West pork pie

Chicken pot pies

Pot pies are a great way to 'dress up' any casserole. I have used a quick and easy chicken mixture here, but you could use almost any casserole from this book for the filling.

Pre-rolled flaky pastry sheets make life easy, but the exact quantity required depends on the shape and size of the containers you use. (This recipe makes enough filling for four 350ml bowls which are about 11cm across.)

For 4 servings:
2 tablespoons olive (or canola) oil
2 medium (350g trimmed total) leeks, sliced
2–3 cloves garlic, crushed, peeled and chopped
250–300g button mushrooms, halved or quartered
400g boneless skinless chicken breasts or thighs, cubed
1 tablespoon fresh thyme
½ cup each dry white wine and cream
½–1 teaspoon salt
black pepper to taste
2–4 sheets pre-rolled puff (flaky) pastry, thawed
1 egg plus 1 tablespoon water, lightly beaten

Heat the oil in a large non-stick pan. Add the leeks and garlic and cook, stirring frequently, until the leeks are soft (about 5 minutes). Stir in the mushrooms and continue to cook until these have just softened, then add the chicken and stir-fry until the chicken has lost its pink colour.

Add the thyme, wine and cream and simmer for 10–12 minutes or until the chicken is cooked through. Season to taste with salt and pepper. Prepare the filling in advance if desired.

Preheat the oven to 200°C. Place the pastry sheets on a dry lightly floured bench and cut four rounds, slightly larger (about 1cm) than the tops of your selected bowls/ramekins. Cut the trimmings into strips about 1.5cm wide.

Divide the filling between the four containers, filling each to about 1cm below the rim. Brush the rims lightly with water, then make a ring of the pastry strips around the top of each dish, pressing them down gently. Lightly brush the pastry-covered rims with water then top with the pasty rounds to make a lid. Gently press around the edges, fluting them if desired. Decorate the tops with pastry trimmings if desired.

Using the point of a sharp knife, carefully poke a vent in the centre of each pie, then brush the tops lightly with the beaten egg mixture. Place pies in the oven and bake at 200°C for 15–20 minutes or until the tops are golden brown. Serve alone or accompany with a salad or lightly cooked vegetables and a slice or two of French bread.

Easy tomato and feta 'tart'

This easy 'tart' is really a very close relative of pizza. It looks and tastes great, but since it uses bought, pre-rolled pastry it really couldn't be much simpler to prepare.

For 4 servings:
2 sheets (about 300g) pre-rolled flaky pastry, thawed
2 tablespoons tomato paste
1 teaspoon dried basil or 1 tablespoon pesto
1 tablespoon water
½ teaspoon each marjoram and salt
grind of black pepper
250g small ripe tomatoes
1 small or ½ medium red onion
½ medium yellow or red capsicum, deseeded
1 medium zucchini
1–2 cloves garlic, crushed, peeled and chopped
about 8 basil leaves, roughly shredded
2 tablespoons olive oil
100g feta cheese, crumbled
salt and pepper to taste

Preheat the oven to 200°C.

Lay the first sheet of pastry on a lightly oiled or non-stick sprayed baking sheet. Brush the surface lightly with water then lay the second sheet exactly on top. Roll or press the two sheets lightly together. Without cutting right through the pastry run a sharp knife around the sheet about 1.5–2cm inside the edge, marking out a smaller square.

Mix together the tomato paste, dried basil or pesto, water, marjoram, salt and black pepper. Spread this paste evenly over the surface of the smaller square, trying to keep the edge clean. Cut each of the tomatoes and the onion into 6–8 small wedges and slice the capsicum into strips about 1cm wide. Halve the zucchini lengthwise and cut into thin (5mm) ribbons.

Combine the vegetables, garlic (if using) and basil leaves in a plastic bag or bowl. Add the olive oil and stir gently until they are well mixed and evenly coated with oil.

Arrange the prepared vegetables over the paste-covered base, then sprinkle the tart evenly with crumbled feta. Season with salt and pepper to taste, then bake at 200°C for 20–25 minutes, or until the crust is golden brown.

Serve hot, warm or cold with a green salad or as part of a picnic buffet.

Chicken pot pies

Spinach and feta pie

This very simple pie is loosely based on Greek Spanakopita – it is another great example of how filo pastry can be used to make a dramatic looking dish with a minimum of effort. It can be served hot, warm or cold and is great as part of a summer picnic.

For 4–6 servings:
1 tablespoon olive oil
1 medium onion
¼ cup pine nuts
500g frozen spinach, thawed and drained
200g feta cheese, crumbled
¼ teaspoon each dried basil and thyme
¼ – ½ teaspoon freshly grated nutmeg
½ –1 teaspoon salt
black pepper to taste
2 eggs
10 sheets filo pastry
about 2 tablespoons melted butter or olive oil

Heat the oil in a medium-sized frypan, add the onion and cook until softened. Stir in the pine nuts and continue to cook until these are golden brown.

While the onion cooks, squeeze as much liquid as you can from the thawed spinach. Place the spinach in a large bowl and add the crumbled cheese, then the herbs, seasonings and the onion-pine nut mixture. (The quantity of salt required will depend on the saltiness of the feta – vary it to taste.) Add the eggs and stir until well mixed.

Turn the oven on to preheat to 200°C, and non-stick spray or oil a shallow casserole dish (about 20 x 25cm). Lay two sheets of filo out on the bench, and brush the top sheet lightly with melted butter or olive oil. Lay these sheets lengthwise down the prepared dish, gently pressing them into the bottom, leaving the edges overhanging. Prepare another two sheets and lay these in the dish at right angles to the first sheets. Repeat this process so that there are eight sheets of filo in the dish.

Gently spread the spinach filling mix over the pastry in the bottom of the dish. Cover the spinach mixture with the remaining two sheets of filo, folded to make them fit. Fold in the overhanging edges of the bottom sheets, and lightly brush the surface with oil or melted butter.

Bake at 200°C for 20–25 minutes until golden brown and firm when pressed in the centre. Serve hot, warm or even cold.

Note:

If you prefer, you can use the filling mixture to make 10–12 smaller filo triangles. Lay one sheet of filo on a dry surface and brush it lightly with oil, then fold in half lengthwise. Place about ¼ cup of the filling mixture close to one end, then fold the corner up diagonally to cover the filling (so the bottom edge meets the side). Keep folding the filling (straight then diagonally) until you reach the end of the strip. Fold any extra pastry under the package, brush lightly with oil or melted butter and place on a baking tray. Repeat until all the filling is used. Bake as above, but reduce cooking time to 12–15 minutes.

Pizzas

Pizzas are an excellent one-dish meal. There are many different options but, at their simplest, it is just a matter of tossing a few selected toppings (even a collection of leftovers from the fridge) onto a bought or home-made base, and baking!

These days it seems that almost anything goes when it comes to pizza toppings. While it has to be said that some complex topping combinations can work well, I think relatively simple combinations tend to work the best.

For 1 very large, 2 medium, or 8 individual pizzas:
1 recipe bread base (see next page)
1 recipe easy tomato topping (see next page)

Then add your selection of:
a little thinly sliced onion
thinly sliced red/green/yellow capsicums
sliced mushrooms
sliced or diced ham/bacon, salami, sliced cooked sausages, shredded chicken, assorted seafood or surimi, etc.
thin slices or wedges of tomato (or halved cherry tomatoes)
roasted vegetables (tomatoes, mushrooms, capsicums, eggplant, zucchini etc.)
anchovies and/or chopped olives
chopped fresh or dried basil, thyme etc.
250–400g sliced, grated, or crumbled cheese (mild or tasty cheddar, mozzarella, feta, or a mixture)
olive oil to drizzle (optional)

Preheat the oven to 200°C while you assemble your pizza/s. Place the base/s on a lightly oiled (or teflon lined) oven slide or pizza tray. Start by spreading the base/s with a thin layer of tomato topping, then add your selection of the suggested toppings (2–3 are generally plenty).

Top with a generous layer of sliced, grated, or crumbled cheese and, if you like, drizzle lightly with olive oil.

Bake at 200°C for 10–15 minutes, or until the base has browned underneath.

Easy bread pizza base

Home-made yeasted pizza bases are hard to beat, and are really very easy to prepare, particularly if you have a breadmaker.

For 1 very large, 2 medium, or 8 individual bases:
2 teaspoons active dried yeast
1 cup plus 2 tablespoons warm water
2 teaspoons sugar
1 teaspoon salt
2 tablespoons olive oil
3 cups high grade flour

If using a bread machine: Measure all ingredients into the bowl, set to the dough cycle and start the machine. Check the dough after 5 minutes of mixing to see if it has formed a smoothish round ball, add a little extra flour (1–2 tablespoons) if the dough looks sticky or 1–2 tablespoons water if the dough looks too dry. If you are in a particular hurry you can remove the dough anytime after about 40 minutes of mixing, otherwise leave to the end of the cycle. Shape as described below.

If making by hand: Measure the first five ingredients and 1 cup of the flour into a large bowl and mix until well combined. Cover the bowl and leave to stand in a warm place for 15 minutes, then stir in the remaining flour (adding a little extra if necessary) to make a dough just firm enough to knead. Knead for 10 minutes, then cover and leave in a warm place to rise until doubled in size.

Turn dough onto a floured surface and divide as required then roll each piece into a thin (5–7mm) round shape. Place in pizza pans or a baking sheet, then top and bake as described for 'Pizzas' on this page.

Easy tomato topping

This mixture is more interesting than straight tomato purée or paste, and almost as easy as a bought pizza topping!

For about ½ cup:
½ cup tomato paste
1 teaspoon garlic salt
½ teaspoon dried basil or oregano
2–3 tablespoons water
black pepper

Measure the tomato paste, garlic salt and basil or oregano into a small bowl and mix, adding enough water to make an easily spreadable paste. Add pepper to taste.

Calzone and Stromboli

If you do make your own pizza bases, why not try something a little different with these 'closed' pizzas.

Calzone
Arrange pizza fillings over one half of (individual-sized) base/s, leaving 2cm uncovered at the edge. Moisten round the edge, then fold the uncovered half over the filled half to make a half moon shape, pressing the edges together. Bake like a pizza.

Stromboli
Roll 1 recipe of the Easy Bread Pizza Base (this page) into 2 large (50 x 75cm), very thin rectangle/s. Top like pizza (use toppings sparingly), leaving a 5cm strip at one of the short edges uncovered. Brush the uncovered edge lightly with water, then starting at the other short edge, roll the dough up like a sponge roll.

Place the roll on a baking sheet so it sits seam-side down, then slash the top diagonally a couple of times to prevent splitting and bake as for pizza.

Tomato, basil and mozzarella pizza

While I have nothing against 'Americanised' pizzas, there is something remarkably delicious about simpler, more traditional Italian-style pizzas – this recipe is a case in point. The ingredients look so simple it seems unlikely that it could taste as good as it does!

For 2–3 servings:
½ recipe Easy Bread Pizza Base (see page 31)
about ¼ cup Easy Tomato Topping (see page 31)
2 medium firm ripe tomatoes
        (or 15–20 cherry tomatoes, halved)
15–20 fresh basil leaves
100–150g mozzarella cheese, in 5mm slices
about 1 tablespoon olive oil
black pepper

Preheat oven to 200°C.

Roll dough out into an oval about 25 x 40cm. Spread thinly with the tomato topping, leaving 1–2cm uncovered around the edges (you can leave these as they are or brush lightly with water and fold them in if you like).

Quarter the tomatoes, then cut each quarter into 3 thin wedges. Scatter the tomato wedges (or halved cherry tomatoes) over the base, then arrange the basil leaves evenly over the pizza (tearing any large leaves into 2–3 smaller pieces).

Arrange the mozzarella slices over the surface, then drizzle the pizza with about 1 tablespoon olive oil and sprinkle with black pepper.

Bake at 200°C for 12–15 minutes, or until the cheese is golden brown.

Cheese and mushroom flan

Flans or quiches seem to have slipped from favour a little at present, but they form a good basis for a meal, and are relatively quick and easy to prepare, even if you make your own pastry.

For a 23–25cm flan (4 servings):
Pastry
1 cup plain flour
75g cold butter, cubed
¼ cup water acidulated with 2 teaspoons lemon juice

Filling
2 tablespoons olive (or canola) oil
1 medium onion, diced
200g mushrooms, sliced
1 teaspoon fresh thyme, chopped (½ teaspoon dried)
1½ –2 cups grated gruyere (or cheddar) cheese
3 large eggs
½ cup lite or regular sour cream
¼ cup milk
½ teaspoon salt
paprika to dust

Pastry
Measure the flour and cold butter into a food processor fitted with a metal chopping blade. Begin adding the acidulated water in a thin stream while chopping the butter through the flour in short bursts. Stop at intervals and see if the particles are moist enough to press together to form a dough. As soon as you can press the crumbs into a ball remove the dough from the processor. Cover and refrigerate until required.

Working on a lightly floured surface, roll the dough out to fit a 23–25cm pie or flan dish.

Filling
Preheat the oven to 220°C.

Heat the oil in a medium-sized non-stick pan, then add the onion, mushrooms and thyme and sauté until softened.

Cover the bottom of the uncooked crust with the grated cheese, then cover this with the onion and mushroom mixture. Beat the eggs, sour cream, milk and salt together, then pour into the crust.

Dust the surface with paprika, then bake at 220°C for about 30 minutes or until the filling is firm in the centre.

Serve with crusty bread and a green salad.

Variations:
The possible variations on this flan are almost limitless. Try mixing the cheese with the egg-sour cream mixture and replacing the mushroom mixture with 1–2 cups of other cooked (or drained canned) vegetables or combination of vegetables and a small (about 200g) drained can of salmon or tuna. Some good combinations include:

asparagus and cheese
smoked salmon and potato
spinach and cheese
tuna and spring onion
spinach and tuna

Tomato, basil and mozzarella pizza

Empañadas

Empañadas are little pies, presumably of Spanish origin. They are now common as fast or take-away food in Central and South America.

I have given two options, the first is meat based and requires pre-cooking and the other is a simpler vegetarian option.

Pastry for 8 empañadas (4 servings):

3 cups plain flour
½ teaspoon salt
½ cup canola oil
½ cup yoghurt
2–3 tablespoons water, if required

Make the pastry first so it can stand while you prepare the filling. Measure the flour, salt, and oil into the bowl of a food processor. Process in short bursts until the mixture looks like breadcrumbs. Add the yoghurt and process again in a few short bursts, then test to see if the mixture will press together to form a dough. If not, add the water 1 tablespoon at a time, processing briefly between each addition, until it does. Avoid over-mixing as this will make the dough tough. Cover the dough and refrigerate while you prepare the filling.

Meat-based Filling

2 tablespoons olive (or canola) oil
1 medium onion, finely diced
2 cloves garlic, peeled and chopped
1 red or green capsicum, deseeded and diced
250g minced lamb or beef
2 teaspoons ground cumin
½ teaspoon each paprika, cinnamon and chilli powder
½ cup frozen peas or corn (optional)
¼ cup chopped green or black olives
1 tablespoon tomato paste
2 tablespoons dry white wine, lemon (or lime) juice
2 hard-boiled eggs, roughly chopped
2–3 tablespoons chopped parsley
salt and pepper to taste

Heat the oil in a large pan. Add the onion and garlic and cook, stirring frequently for about 2 minutes. Stir in the capsicum and minced lamb or beef and continue to cook, stirring frequently, until the meat has lost its pink colour. Add the seasonings, peas or corn (if using), chopped olives, tomato paste and wine or juice.

Reduce the heat and cook, stirring occasionally, for about 5 minutes longer, then remove from the heat. Stir the hard-boiled eggs and parsley into the meat mixture. Season to taste with salt and pepper.

Vegetarian Filling

2 cups (200g) grated tasty cheese
2 hard-boiled eggs, chopped
1 large red or green capsicum, deseeded and diced
¼ cup chopped green or black olives
1 tablespoon capers, chopped (optional)
1 teaspoon ground cumin
½ teaspoon each chilli powder and oregano

Measure all the ingredients into a large bowl and mix well.

To make the empañadas

Divide the dough into eight equal pieces. Shape each piece into a round ball, then working one piece at a time on a lightly floured surface (loosely cover the remaining pieces to prevent drying), roll out to form a 12cm disc.

Place ¼ cup of the filling mixture in the middle then moisten around the edge with a little water and fold the dough in half, making a half moon shape. Press the edges together to seal, using your fingers or the tines of a fork.

Repeat this process until you have eight little packages. Arrange these on a lightly oiled (or baking paper covered) baking sheet and lightly brush with oil. Bake at 180°C for 25–30 minutes or until golden brown.

Serve warm or cold with chilli sauce or salsa.

Filo fish roll

This very easy and attractive filo roll is an unusual and different way to use some of the lesser regarded (and cheaper) varieties of fish like hoki.

For 4 servings:

½ cup regular or lite sour cream
1 tablespoon horseradish sauce
finely grated rind of ½ lemon
1–2 tablespoons chopped fresh dill (1 teaspoon dried)
½ –1 teaspoon salt
8 sheets filo pastry
2 tablespoons olive oil or melted butter
400–500g fish fillets, sliced 1cm thick
½ each red and green capsicum, deseeded and diced
1–2 sticks celery, diced
black pepper to taste

Preheat the oven to 200°C.

Measure the sour cream, horseradish sauce, lemon rind, dill and salt to taste into a small bowl and mix well.

Lay two sheets of filo pastry on a clean, dry surface and brush the top sheet lightly with oil or melted butter, add another two sheets and oil or butter again. Repeat this process until you have a stack eight sheets thick.

Spread the sour cream mixture over the filo sheets, leaving a 5cm strip of pastry visible at one of the short ends. Arrange the sliced fish evenly over the sour cream-covered part, then scatter the vegetables evenly over the fish. Sprinkle with black pepper.

Roll the filo up like a sponge roll, finishing so the roll rests on the uncovered portion of the filo.

Place the roll on a non-stick sprayed or baking paper (or teflon) lined sponge roll tin and brush the outside with oil or melted butter. Place the roll in the oven and bake for 30–40 minutes or until the filo is golden brown. Remove from the oven and leave to stand for 10–15 minutes before serving.

Serve accompanied by a green salad and rice or pasta if desired.

Spinach, rice and blue cheese torte

Even if you don't like spinach, you'll love this versatile and unusual torte! It looks great and can be served hot, warm or cool, making it suitable for any meal from a picnic to an elegant lunch or dinner.

It is a little more substantial made with brown rice, but this does take considerably longer to cook, so I often make a decision on which to use based on how much time I have available.

For 4 servings:

1 cup rice, brown or white
1 tablespoon olive (or canola) oil
1 medium onion, diced
250g frozen spinach, thawed
½ teaspoon basil
½ teaspoon marjoram
1 teaspoon salt
black pepper to taste
1 cup (250g) cottage cheese
100–125g creamy blue cheese, crumbled or cubed
3 large eggs, lightly beaten
2–3 tomatoes, thinly sliced

Bring a large pot of water to the boil and add the rice. Boil until the rice is just tender: 8–10 minutes for white rice or 12–15 minutes for brown rice, then drain well.

While the rice cooks, heat the oil in a large pot or pan. Add the diced onion and cook until the onion is soft and clear. Gently squeeze the thawed spinach to get rid of excess liquid, then add this to the pan along with the herbs, salt and a generous grind of black pepper. Cook for 1–2 minutes longer, then remove from the heat.

Mix in the drained rice, cottage cheese, blue cheese, and lightly beaten eggs.

Line a 22–25cm round springform cake tin with baking paper or a teflon liner, then spoon in the rice mixture and smooth the top. Arrange a layer of sliced tomatoes over the surface and bake at 180°C for 40 minutes. Remove from the oven and cool for about 10 minutes before removing from the tin.

Serve hot, warm or cool with bread and a salad, or lightly cooked seasonal vegetables.

Lamb souvlaki

Pita pockets stuffed with this tasty marinated lamb and salad make a great easy meal. The lamb cubes can be cooked 'loose' or skewered like kebabs, either under the grill or on the barbecue.

I like to use pita breads that are about 12–15cm across, splitting them and stuffing the pockets with the lamb and salads, but if you want, you can use larger ones, rolling them round the filling rather than stuffing it into the pocket. Once again, this is a dish well suited to being assembled by diners at the table, so all you need to do is get everything together.

For 2–3 servings:

1 small-medium onion
3 cloves garlic
3 tablespoons olive oil
1 teaspoon each cumin and thyme
½ teaspoon each oregano and chilli powder
½ –1 teaspoon ground black pepper
350–400g lean cubed lamb

To serve:

½ cup plain unsweetened yoghurt mixed with 2 tablespoons
    lemon or lime juice and ½ teaspoon paprika
about 2 cups shredded lettuce
about ¼ cup thinly sliced red onion
tabouleh (see page 46)
4–6 pita breads

Measure the first eight ingredients into a food processor or blender and process to form a smooth paste. Place the lamb in a bowl (or plastic bag) then add the marinade paste and stir until the meat is well covered. Leave to stand for at least 20 minutes, or preferably longer. (For a really good flavour, the marinade and lamb can be mixed the night before and refrigerated until required.)

Thread the marinated lamb onto skewers (if desired), or arrange the cubes on a foil-covered baking sheet. Place 5–10cm from a hot grill and cook (or barbecue) for about 5–7 minutes, turning occasionally until the outside begins to blacken slightly but the inside remains a little pink. Allow the cooked meat to stand for about 5 minutes before serving.

While the lamb cooks, prepare the sauce, lettuce, onion and tabouleh (see page 46).

To serve:

Brush the pita breads with a little water or oil if they feel dry, then warm them by microwaving for 15–20 seconds each. Halve and split the pita breads (if desired). Fill each with a little shredded lettuce, some tabouleh, a few onion slices and 6–8 cubes of lamb. Add a spoonful or two of the sauce and serve. (There is no tidy way to eat these – fingers work best so provide plenty of napkins or paper towels.)

Lamb souvlaki

Seekh kebabs

Seekh Kebabs are made from seasoned minced lamb, shaped into 'sausages' which are then skewered for support and cooked. You can make them smaller and serve as an entrée, but they make a good main course when served on rice or with flat bread and a salad.

For 3–4 servings (8–12 kebabs):
½ medium onion
2 cloves garlic, peeled
2–3cm piece fresh ginger
500g minced lamb
1 teaspoon each ground cumin, coriander, garam masala and dried mint
1 teaspoon salt
½ teaspoon each chilli powder, ground cloves and cinnamon
8–12 wooden skewers (soaked in cold water)

Place the onion, garlic and ginger in a food processor and process until very finely chopped (or mince very finely by hand).

Add the minced lamb and seasonings then process (or mix by hand) until combined. Knead in the processor, or by hand, until it has a smooth even consistency. (This kneading changes the texture of the mince and ensures that the 'sausages' do not break up during cooking.)

Divide the mixture into quarters, then each quarter into 2 or 3 smaller portions. With wet hands, shape each piece into a sausage 2–3cm thick and 10–12cm long. Spear each of these lengthwise with a skewer. Leave 'sausages' in a round shape or flatten each one gently between your hands.

Grill close to the heat for 4–5 minutes each side, or until nicely browned and no longer pink in the middle.

Serve as an entrée, or as the main part of a meal accompanied with rice and/or naan (or other flat bread) and a salad. Spoon Herbed Yoghurt Sauce over them, if you like.

Herbed Yoghurt Sauce

1 cup plain unsweetened yoghurt
2–3 tablespoons finely chopped fresh mint
about ¼ cup chopped fresh coriander
1 tablespoon lemon or lime juice
½ teaspoon salt

Mix all ingredients together and leave to stand for at least 15 minutes.

Quick chicken satay sticks

Thin strips of breast meat threaded on skewers are very quick to cook and look exotic when served. This is a great way to turn a couple of chicken breasts into a quick, interesting meal.

For 2 servings:
2 boneless, skinless chicken breasts, each cut into 5–6 strips
1–2 tablespoons lemon (or lime) juice
1 tablespoon each soy sauce and fish sauce
1–2 teaspoons sesame oil
1 teaspoon ground cumin
2 cloves garlic, crushed, peeled and chopped
1 teaspoon grated fresh ginger
1 tablespoon chopped coriander leaves (optional)
10–12 wooden skewers (soaked in cold water)

Place the chicken strips in a bag with all the ingredients. Leave to marinate for at least 5 minutes or up to 24 hours. (Refrigerate if marinating for more than 20 minutes.) Thread the chicken strips lengthwise onto the skewers and grill or barbecue close to the heat until cooked, 3–5 minutes each side (juice should run clear when chicken is pierced).

Serve on rice with warm (bought or home-made) Satay Sauce (below) and a cucumber or other salad. It crosses some cultural boundaries, but I think Malaysian-style roti also goes well too.

Quick Satay Sauce

2 tablespoons canola oil
1 onion, chopped
1 clove garlic, crushed, peeled and chopped
½ teaspoon minced red chilli or chilli powder
2 teaspoons brown sugar
1 teaspoon grated fresh ginger
1 tablespoon dark soy sauce
2 tablespoons lemon juice
½ cup peanut butter
about ½ cup water
leftover chicken cooking juices from above
salt to taste

Heat the oil in a medium-sized pan over a moderate heat. Add the onion and garlic and cook until the onion is transparent. Stir in the next six ingredients. Add the water and any remaining marinade and cooking juices, bring to the boil, then season to taste with salt. Thin to pouring consistency with extra water. Refrigerate leftovers, thinning with extra water before serving.

Rice paper rolls

These rice paper rolls are simple and delicious. You can buy the rice papers (from some supermarkets or Asian food stores) in various sizes, so you can make little rolls in advance and serve them with drinks, or let diners assemble their own rolls at the table using larger wrappers.

For 3–4 servings:
½ cup water
¼ cup light soy sauce
2 tablespoons brown sugar
2 tablespoons sherry
2 cloves garlic, chopped
1 tablespoon grated ginger
½ teaspoon five spice powder
300–400g boneless, skinless chicken breasts
12–16 rice paper wrappers

Combine the first seven ingredients in a frypan or pot, heat to boiling, then add the chicken and simmer gently, turning once or twice for about 15 minutes, or until the chicken is cooked through. Remove from the heat and leave the chicken to cool in the cooking liquid.

Shred the cooled chicken, place in a small bowl and toss with 1–2 tablespoons of cooking liquid. (Store in fridge if preparing in advance).

While the chicken cools, prepare dipping sauce (see below). Gather together (or place in bowls if you are serving at the table) extra fillings for the rolls. My favourites are chopped mint leaves and/or coriander leaves, bean sprouts, finely shredded lettuce, grated carrot, chopped peanuts and chives.

To make each roll, soak a wrapper in warm water until soft and white (about 15 seconds). Lift out and lie flat. Place some shredded chicken and your choice of extras on the wrapper. Fold in the edges then roll up to make a little parcel. Dip into the sauce below and enjoy!

Dipping Sauce
juice of 1 lime
¼ cup each water and fish sauce
1 tablespoon caster sugar
2 cloves garlic, finely chopped
1 small red chilli, finely chopped (optional)

Combine all ingredients in a small bowl and leave to stand for at least 5 minutes.

Sang chow bow (lettuce leaf parcels)

Crisp lettuce leaves stuffed with this moist, flavourful pork mixture are almost irresistible.

To keep the lettuce crisp, the parcels really need to be assembled at the table, but I think this only adds to their appeal.

For 4 servings:
2 tablespoons canola oil
2–3 cloves garlic, crushed, peeled and chopped
500g minced pork
100–150g mushrooms, chopped
½–1 teaspoon minced chilli (optional)
1 tablespoon each rice wine (or sherry),
    oyster sauce and hoi sin sauce
1–2 tablespoons Kikkoman soy sauce
¼ cup chopped fresh basil, mint or coriander
    (or mixture)
1 iceberg lettuce

Heat the oil in a large non-stick pan, add the garlic and minced pork and cook, stirring frequently, until the pork is lightly browned. Add the mushrooms and chilli and cook for a further 3–5 minutes.

Add the next four ingredients. Stir to mix, then reduce the heat and simmer gently for 8–10 minutes. Remove from heat and stir in the chopped herbs.

Leave the mince mixture to cool while you separate the lettuce into individual leaves. Divide mixture between 4 small dishes or place mixture in one large serving bowl and surround with lettuce leaves.

To eat, wrap a small quantity of mince mixture in a lettuce leaf. If you feel the need for something extra, serve accompanied with steamed rice, which can be added to the parcels or eaten on its own.

Sushi

Sushi is definitely not a new idea, but is becoming an increasingly popular meal option. Instead of thinking of sushi as just a starter, try making several different shapes and varieties and serving them as a main course.

The name sushi actually refers to the vinegared rice mixture, but what makes it so interesting and delicious are the fillings and presentation. Obviously exactly which ingredients you will need vary depending on the end product/s you want to make, but I have suggested some of my favourite fillings below.

For 3–4 main course servings:
2 cups short-grain rice
3½ cups boiling water
3 tablespoons each rice vinegar and sugar
2 tablespoons sherry
2 teaspoons salt

To microwave:

Place the rice in a large microwave-proof bowl and cover with cold water. Drain the rice, then cover with water and drain again.

Pour the boiling water over the rice, then cover the bowl and microwave at medium (50%) power for 15–20 minutes or until the rice is completely tender. Remove the bowl from the microwave and stir in the vinegar, sugar, sherry and salt. Leave rice to cool to room temperature.

To cook conventionally:

Place the rice in a large heavy pot (with a close-fitting lid), then cover with cold water. Drain the rice, then cover with water and drain again.

Measure in the boiling water, bring rice to the boil, then cover pot and reduce the heat to very low and leave to steam for 15 minutes. Remove the pot from the heat and stand for a further 10 minutes before stirring in the vinegar, sugar, sherry and salt. Leave rice to cool to room temperature.

Which fillings you choose will depend on the type of sushi you are making and your own preferences, but here are a few suggestions:

strips of cucumber
strips of carrot
sliced avocado
strips of red/green/yellow capsicum
smoked (or raw) salmon
strips of omelette
shredded surimi
fresh (or canned) tuna
pickled ginger
pickled vegetables
wasabi paste
yaki nori (roasted seaweed sheets)

Rolled Sushi (Maki-zushi)

Probably the best-known form of sushi, sliced sushi rolls are actually very easy to make. Lay a sheet of nori on a clean dry bench or sushi mat (the mat is not essential but does make getting the roll started a little easier). Spread a layer of rice about 1cm thick over the nori, leaving a 2–3cm strip down one long edge clear.

Arrange your selected fillings in a band along the middle of the rice, brush the exposed nori strip with a little water, then starting from the rice-covered edge, roll up your sushi. Sit the roll seam side down for 2–3 minutes before cutting into 2–3cm thick slices.

Hand Rolls (Temaki-zushi)

Cut a sheet of nori in half lengthwise. Place one strip on the bench and spread a heaped tablespoon of rice diagonally across one end and arrange a few strips of your selected filling on top of the rice. Fold the exposed corner across the fillings, then roll the sheet up to form a cone. Repeat to make as many hand rolls as you want.

Moulded Sushi (Nigiri-zushi)

This has to be the simplest sushi to make. Moisten your (clean!) hands then press a heaped tablespoon of rice into the palm of one hand. Squeeze and shape the rice until it is flat on the bottom and curved on the top (adjust the size to suit the size of the fish you will use). Spread one side of a thinly sliced piece of raw (or cold smoked) salmon or tuna with wasabi, then place it wasabi side down over the curved side of the rice. Decorate with a thin 'belt' of nori if desired.

To serve, arrange your sushi on plates or a platter and serve accompanied with pickled ginger, a little wasabi paste and a bowl of Kikkoman soy sauce for dipping.

Asian-style pork patties

If you make hamburgers regularly and want to make something a little different, try this delicious Asian-flavoured version.

The shape doesn't really matter, but I like to make them oblong or oval and serve them in long buns to emphasise that they are something a little different.

For 4 servings:
1 cup (2–3 thick slices) breadcrumbs
250–300g pork mince
2 cloves garlic, crushed, peeled and chopped
1–2cm fresh ginger, finely grated
1 egg
½–1 teaspoon minced chilli (optional)
2 teaspoons sesame oil
1 tablespoon Kikkoman soy sauce
½ teaspoon salt
2–3 tablespoons chopped fresh coriander

Place all ingredients in a large bowl and mix thoroughly (clean hands work best for this). Divide the mixture into 4 balls, then flatten these into long oval patties – it doesn't matter if they're not perfect.

Cook in a hot lightly oiled pan, lightly browning both sides, then lower the heat and cook until centre is firm – barbecue instead if you prefer.

Serve in lightly toasted hotdog buns or French bread with Oriental Coleslaw (below).

Oriental Coleslaw

Dressing

2 tablespoons canola oil
1 tablespoon each Kikkoman soy sauce, sweet chilli sauce and rice wine (or wine) vinegar
1 teaspoon sesame oil

Salad

2 cups shredded cabbage
2–3 sticks celery, thinly sliced
1 medium carrot, grated
1–2 spring onions, thinly sliced
handful bean sprouts (optional)
chopped peanuts (optional)

To make dressing, measure all ingredients into a screw-top jar and shake to combine.

Put the vegetables in a large bowl and toss to combine, adding just enough dressing to moisten everything (extra dressing will keep well in the fridge). Serve as described with Asian-style Pork Patties, or as a side salad.

Home-made hamburgers

My wife and I have just rediscovered home-made hamburgers. Not only are they quick and easy to prepare, but they taste great and are popular with children. It sounds like a cliché, but hot off your own stove they really are quite different to anything you can buy.

For 4 'quarter-pound' burgers:
500g minced beef
1 cup (2–3 slices bread) soft breadcrumbs
1 large egg
1 teaspoon garlic salt
black pepper to taste

Place all the ingredients in a large bowl, then mix thoroughly (clean hands work best for this). Divide the mixture into 4 balls then flatten these into roundish patties – it doesn't matter if they're not perfectly round.

Grill or barbecue about 20cm from the heat, turning when browned, or, brown on both sides in a hot, lightly oiled frypan, then lower heat and cook until the centre is firm when pressed.

Serve in lightly toasted plain or sesame buns with 3 or 4 of the following:

sliced tomato
torn or shredded lettuce (or coleslaw)
sliced cheese
fried egg
red, yellow and green capsicums (raw or roasted)
sautéed mushrooms
sliced gherkins or dill pickles
thinly sliced red onion, crisped by soaking in cold water
sliced avocado
sliced beetroot
watercress or other fresh herbs
chilli beans and sour cream

Of course no burger is complete without tomato sauce and/or mustard.

Home-made hamburger

Tacos, tostadas, burritos and nachos

Spicy Mexican Filling

This spicy mince and bean mixture can be used as the basis of any of the Mexican-style treats described below. It is quick to make, and leftovers freeze well.

For 2–4 servings:
1 tablespoon olive or canola oil
1 large red onion, diced
2 cloves garlic, crushed, peeled and chopped
250g minced beef
1 red or green capsicum, deseeded and diced
1 teaspoon each salt and sugar
½ –1 teaspoon chilli powder
2 teaspoons ground cumin
1 teaspoon oregano
440g can kidney beans, drained and rinsed
2 tablespoons tomato paste
¼ – ½ cup water

Heat the oil in a large non-stick pan, add the onion, garlic and minced beef and cook over fairly high heat until browned. Add the capsicum, salt and sugar, and spices, and cook for a further 2 minutes.

Reduce the heat, add the beans, tomato paste and ¼ cup water and stir. Simmer for 10–15 minutes, stirring occasionally to prevent sticking. Add extra water during this time if the mixture begins to look dry.

Tacos and Tostadas

Taco shells are corn tortillas that are fried or baked until crisp and folded into a U shape. A tostada is simply a tortilla (usually corn), cooked in the same way, but left flat. Instead of being filled, like tacos, tostadas simply have the same 'fillings' piled on top.

To serve tacos or tostadas, you can either give everyone their own shells and have them help themselves from bowls of fillings, or assemble them yourself before serving.

Fillings:
Spicy Mexican Filling (above)
grated cheese
very finely shredded lettuce
finely grated carrot

Optional extras:
sliced mushrooms
chopped olives
diced tomatoes
diced capsicums (or chillies)
sliced avocado (or guacamole)
sour cream
chilli sauce or salsa
chopped fresh coriander
sliced spring onions

I have given the fillings above in the order that I like to add them, i.e. start with the mince mixture then add cheese, then lettuce etc., finishing with guacamole, sour cream and/or chilli sauce.

Be warned, there is no neat way to eat tacos or tostadas – use your fingers and accept that a little mess is part of the fun!

Burritos

A burrito is simply a soft flour tortilla wrapped around your selected fillings. They can be bought in various sizes from fairly small (about 20cm across) to quite large (about 40cm across).

Fillings for burritos are exactly the same as for tacos and tostadas. However, if you are using the large tortillas you may also want to add a little rice.

To fill a burrito, lay the tortilla on a flat surface. Arrange the fillings in a line that runs about ¾ of the way from top to bottom (don't be too generous with the fillings or your burrito will be difficult to roll and almost impossible to eat!).

When you have finished adding fillings, fold the bottom up over the filling, then fold one edge in, followed by the other so the whole thing resembles a tall skinny envelope. (Wrapping this whole construction in a napkin will make it easier to eat.)

Nachos

Nachos are always popular and seem to be received with equal enthusiasm by all age groups! In their simplest form they are just corn chips with melted cheese over them, but by adding Spicy Mexican Filling and a few other optional extras, you can turn them into a substantial meal.

corn chips (any flavour)
grated cheese
Spicy Mexican Filling (see above)
optional extras (as for Tacos)

Preheat the grill while you place a pile of the heated mince mixture in the centre of a flat (ovenproof) plate or platter. Pile the corn chips around this, then sprinkle the corn chips liberally with your selected extra toppings and grated cheese. Grill until the cheese has melted. Top with a dollop of sour cream and/or guacamole and a splash of chilli sauce or salsa. Serve immediately.

Fresh corn cakes (or fritters)

Serve these delicious corn cakes (or fritters) topped with the salsa given below, or for something even easier serve them accompanied with sweet chilli sauce.

If fresh corn is in season, use this, but if you want to make them any other time you can use frozen or (well drained) canned whole corn kernels instead.

For 3–4 servings:
Salsa

2 firm ripe tomatoes, deseeded and diced
1 medium avocado, peeled and diced
½ red onion, diced
2 tablespoons chopped fresh coriander
1–2 tablespoons lemon (or lime) juice
1–2 tablespoons sweet chilli sauce
salt and pepper to taste

Cakes or Fritters

1 cup self-raising flour
2 large eggs
½ cup beer (or soda water, milk etc.)
2 tablespoons sweet chilli sauce
1 teaspoon each cumin and paprika
½ teaspoon salt
1½ –2 cups fresh corn kernels (2–3 cobs)
2 spring onions, finely sliced
2–3 tablespoons chopped coriander
1 medium red or green capsicum, deseeded and diced
oil to fry (see below)

To make the salsa:
Toss the tomatoes, avocado, onion and coriander together in a small bowl. Add enough lemon (or lime) juice and chilli sauce to moisten thoroughly then stir. Season to taste with salt and pepper, then leave to stand while you cook the fritters.

To make the fritters:
Measure the flour into a medium-sized bowl. Add the eggs, beer (or other liquid), chilli sauce, spices and salt, then stir together to make a smooth batter.

Remove the husk and silk from the corn cobs, then slice off the kernels using a sharp knife. Separate then measure the kernels and add to the batter along with the remaining three ingredients.

Heat the oil in a large non-stick pan – for 'traditional' fritters you will need oil 5–10mm deep, or for corn cakes rather than fritters use 1–2 tablespoons.

Cook batches of fritters for 3–5 minutes per side until golden brown, or cakes until they are lightly browned on both sides and firm when pressed in the centre.

Drain cooked fritters on several layers of paper towels. Keep cooked fritters or cakes warm in the oven until all the mixture is cooked, then serve immediately topped with the salsa above, or bowls of sweet chilli sauce.

Cajun beef and bean burgers

These burgers-with-a-twist have several nutritional advantages over conventional burgers – adding the beans effectively lowers the fat content and increases the fibre content at the same time! Perhaps most importantly, they taste great too!

For 4 large or 8 small burgers:
1 slice stale bread (or ½ cup soft breadcrumbs)
½ small onion
1 clove garlic
310g can (1 cup) kidney beans, drained and rinsed
400g lean minced beef
1 teaspoon each cumin, oregano and salt
½ teaspoon each chilli powder, thyme
    and ground black pepper

You can make these burgers by using either of the two following methods, depending whether you want to see or 'hide' the beans!

Put the bread in a food processor fitted with the metal chopping blade and process into fine crumbs, then add the onion and garlic. Process again until finely chopped and well mixed.

For 'invisible' beans add all the beans and process again until they are finely chopped. If you want to see some beans, add only half the beans at this stage. Add the mince and seasonings then process until well mixed. If you reserved any beans, add them at this stage and stir them through the mince mixture, or process again very briefly.

Working with clean wet hands, shape the mixture into 4 large or 8 small patties. Cook and serve as per Home-made Hamburgers (see page 42).

Yoghurt and coriander chicken kebabs

This marinade gives these chicken kebabs an interesting middle-eastern flavour. Serve them with steamed rice and a salad, or consider serving them as a filling to be wrapped in pita or other flat breads.

For 2–3 servings:

Marinade

2 large cloves garlic, crushed, peeled and chopped
2–3 tablespoons chopped fresh coriander
¼ cup plain unsweetened yoghurt
2 tablespoons lemon juice
1 teaspoon finely grated lemon rind
1 teaspoon each paprika and cumin
½ teaspoon salt
¼ – ½ teaspoon chilli powder (optional)

Kebabs

400g boneless skinless chicken breast,
    cut into 2–3cm cubes
6–8 wooden skewers (soaked in cold water)
1 medium red capsicum, deseeded
    and cut into 2cm squares
½ medium red onion, quartered and separated
    (optional)
2 medium zucchini, cut into 1cm slices

Sauce

½ cup plain unsweetened yoghurt
2 tablespoons lemon juice
1–2 tablespoons chopped fresh coriander or mint
1 clove garlic, crushed, peeled and chopped
1 teaspoon paprika
salt to taste

Measure the marinade ingredients into a medium-sized bowl and stir to combine.

Stir the cubed chicken into the marinade, mix until well coated, then cover the bowl with cling film and leave to stand for at least 30 minutes. (Refrigerate if marinating for longer periods.)

Line a shallow baking tray with foil and lightly oil the surface. Thread the chicken and vegetables onto skewers. Start and finish each kebab with a piece of chicken – this will help prevent anything falling off during cooking. Arrange the kebabs on the oiled tray and brush with any remaining marinade.

Turn the grill (or barbecue) on to heat while you prepare the sauce by combining all ingredients in a small bowl.

When the grill (or barbecue) is hot cook kebabs 5–10cm from the heat for 5–7 minutes, then turn and cook for another 5–7 minutes. Check a kebab to ensure the chicken is cooked through (no longer pink in the middle), then remove from the heat.

Serve the kebabs, drizzled with sauce, on steamed rice or tabouleh (see below) with a tomato or green salad, accompanied by warmed flat bread.

Quick couscous tabouleh

Tabouleh is usually made with bulgar (pre-cooked kibbled wheat), but I find couscous works very well instead.

For 1–1½ cups:

½ cup couscous
½ cup boiling water
½ teaspoon instant chicken stock
¼ cup diced deseeded tomato
¼ cup chopped mint (or parsley)
1–2 tablespoons lemon juice
1–2 tablespoons olive oil
salt and pepper to taste

Place the couscous in a small-medium bowl, then add the boiling water and instant stock. Stir, then cover and leave to stand for about 5 minutes.

Fluff the couscous with a fork, add the tomato and mint and stir. Add enough lemon juice and oil to moisten, then season to taste with salt and pepper.

Serve with Lamb Souvlaki (see page 37) or as a salad accompaniment for any Mediterranean-style dish.

Yoghurt and coriander chicken kebabs

Spiced mushroom pilau

Even though I know they really do work well together, every time I look at this recipe I think it seems like an unusual combination of flavours!

It's another longish looking ingredients list, but most of them are added at the same time and everything is cooked in one pan – it is really very simple.

For 3–4 servings:

1½ cups basmati rice
2 tablespoons canola oil
1 large onion, diced
1–2 cloves garlic, crushed, peeled and chopped
2.5cm piece fresh ginger, peeled and chopped
5cm piece cinnamon stick
6 whole cloves
2 cardamom pods, crushed
2 bay leaves
½ teaspoon each mustard seeds and black peppercorns
1 small red chilli, deseeded and chopped (optional)
250g mushrooms, sliced
1 medium red capsicum, deseeded and diced (optional)
500ml boiling water
2 teaspoons mushroom stock powder
½ –1 teaspoon salt
2–3 tablespoons chopped fresh coriander

Measure the rice into a large bowl and cover with cold water and leave to stand for 5–10 minutes.

Heat the oil in a large, preferably lidded, non-stick pan. Add the onion, garlic, ginger, whole spices and the chilli (if using) and cook, stirring frequently, until the onion is soft and is turning clear.

Drain and rinse the rice, then add it to the pan along with the mushrooms and capsicum (if using). Add the boiling water and stock powder and stir until evenly mixed.

Bring the mixture to the boil, then reduce the heat to a very gentle simmer. Cover the pan with a close-fitting lid and cook for 10–15 minutes, stirring every few minutes to prevent sticking, until the rice is tender.

Season to taste with salt, then stir in the fresh coriander and serve.

Spiced mushroom pilau

Paella

I love paella! One of the lasting visions from my overseas travels was seeing a huge (and I mean huge – about 1.5m across) pan of freshly cooked paella for sale at a French market (of all places!). I'm sure given enough time I could have devoured the whole thing.

This recipe may stray a little from its Spanish origin, but one of the 'rules' of paella is that there are no rules! If you have saffron on hand by all means use it, but if you don't, a little turmeric will give a good colour.

For 2–3 large servings:

3 tablespoons olive oil
4 chicken wings or drumsticks
1 medium onion, diced
2–3 cloves garlic, crushed, peeled and chopped
1 green and/or red capsicum, sliced
¾ cup arborio (or calrose) rice
½ teaspoon each paprika, chilli powder and turmeric
    (or saffron strands)
2 cups hot chicken or fish stock (or 2 cups water plus 2
    teaspoons instant stock)
2 tomatoes, cubed
200g assorted seafood (choose any or a combination
    of cubed fish fillets, cooked and peeled shrimp or
    prawns, or sliced squid tubes)
1 cup frozen peas or beans
4–6 small, whole fresh mussels
salt and pepper to taste
2 tablespoons chopped parsley to garnish

Heat 1 tablespoon of the oil in a large pot, pan or wok. Add the chicken pieces and brown on all sides then remove from the pan.

Add the remaining oil, onion and garlic and cook until the onion has softened and slightly browned, stirring occasionally. Stir in the sliced capsicum/s and cook for 1–2 minutes longer, then add the rice. Mix well to ensure all the rice is covered with oil and cook, stirring frequently, until the rice looks milky white.

Stir in the spices, stock and tomatoes, then return the chicken pieces to the pan, cover and bring to the boil. Simmer for about 15 minutes until the chicken and rice are cooked, stirring occasionally so the rice doesn't stick.

Add the seafood of choice and the peas or beans, stir, then top with the mussels. Replace the lid and cook until the mussels open and the fish is opaque, about 3–5 minutes.

Season to taste with salt and pepper, then sprinkle with parsley and serve immediately.

Ham and tomato risotto

Risottos are definitely in my 'what am I going to make for dinner tonight?' repertoire. They are simple and fairly quick to prepare, and most of the ingredients can be kept on hand in the pantry, requiring only fairly minor additions from the fridge or freezer.

This simple risotto is delicious any time of year but there's something about it that always makes me think of summer.

For 2–3 servings:

2 tablespoons olive oil
1 large onion, diced
1 clove garlic, crushed, peeled and chopped
250g ham
1 cup arborio (or calrose) rice
2 cups chicken stock (or water), preferably warm
½ –1 cup hot water (or dry white wine)
3 medium tomatoes, deseeded and diced
¼ cup freshly grated parmesan cheese
¼ cup cream
¼ cup roughly chopped fresh basil
salt and pepper to taste
additional basil and parmesan cheese to garnish

Heat the oil in a large pan, then add the onion and garlic to the pan and cook, stirring frequently to avoid browning, until the onion is soft and turning clear.

While the onion cooks cut the ham into dice or match sticks. Add the ham to the pan and continue to cook until it is lightly browned. Tip in the rice and cook for 2–3 minutes longer, stirring constantly.

Pour in about ½ cup of the stock (or water), and stir constantly until the stock has almost disappeared, then add another ½ cup liquid and repeat, stirring occasionally, until you have used about 2½ cups of liquid.

When the risotto has cooked for about 20 minutes (if the mixture looks too dry add the extra ½ cup of liquid) or the rice is just cooked through (with no hard centres) add the tomatoes, parmesan, cream and chopped basil. Stir to combine and season to taste with salt and pepper.

Heat through, then serve immediately, garnished with freshly grated parmesan and a few basil leaves. Accompany with some crusty bread and a crisp green salad.

Chicken, tomato and basil risotto

Fresh tomatoes give this risotto a lovely pink colour while basil gives it the taste of summer and adds a great contrast of colours.

It's not essential, but peeling the tomatoes does improve the texture by getting rid of rolled up bits of skin. To peel the tomatoes, make a shallow X on the bottom of each, then cover them with boiling water for 20–30 seconds – this should loosen the skin, making it easy to remove.

For 2–3 servings:
1 tablespoon olive oil
2 tablespoons butter
1 medium onion, quartered and sliced
2 cloves garlic, crushed, peeled and chopped
250–300g boneless skinless chicken, sliced or cubed
1½ cups arborio (or calrose) rice
2 large tomatoes, peeled (see above) and diced
2½ cups hot water
2 teaspoons instant chicken stock
1 tablespoon pesto
1–2 teaspoons tomato paste (optional)
3–4 tablespoons coarsely chopped fresh basil
salt and pepper to taste
extra basil leaves to garnish
shaved or grated parmesan cheese (optional)

Heat the oil and butter together in a large pan. Add the onion and garlic to the pan and cook, stirring frequently, until the onion is just beginning to brown.

Add the chicken to the pan and continue to cook until no longer pink, then add the rice and cook for 2–3 minutes longer, stirring constantly.

Add the tomatoes and 1 cup of the water, instant stock and pesto. Bring to the boil, then reduce the heat to a gentle simmer and cook, stirring frequently, until the stock has almost disappeared, then add another ½ cup liquid and repeat, stirring occasionally, until you have used about 2½ cups of liquid. (If you want a pinker colour, add the tomato paste too.)

When the risotto has cooked for about 20 minutes (if the mixture looks too dry add an extra ½ cup liquid) or the rice is just cooked through (with no hard centres) add the chopped basil and season to taste with salt and pepper.

Heat through, then serve immediately, garnished with a few basil leaves and some shaved or grated parmesan (if you want). A crisp green salad and some crusty bread make ideal accompaniments.

Chorizo and capsicum risotto

This is an up-market cousin of the risotto that was a staple for my wife and me as we backpacked round Europe several years ago.

For 3–4 servings:
2 tablespoons olive oil
1 large onion, diced
1 large red capsicum, deseeded and diced
4 (250g total) chorizos, sliced (or diced spicy salami)
1½ cups arborio (or calrose) rice
1 teaspoon thyme
2½ cups hot water
2 teaspoons instant chicken stock
½ cup red or white wine (or additional water)
½–1 cup frozen peas or beans
salt and pepper to taste
shaved or grated parmesan cheese to garnish

Heat the oil in a large, preferably non-stick, frypan. Add the onion and cook, stirring occasionally, until the onion is soft but has not browned. Stir in the diced capsicum and cook until this has softened too, then add the chorizos (or salami) and cook, stirring occasionally, until this begins to brown.

Stir in the rice and thyme and cook for 2–3 minutes longer, stirring constantly. Add 1 cup of the water and the instant stock. Bring to the boil, stirring constantly, then reduce the heat to a gentle simmer and cook, stirring frequently, until the liquid has almost disappeared. Then add another ½ cup liquid and repeat, stirring occasionally, until you have used about 2 cups of water, then add the wine (or additional water).

When the risotto has cooked for about 20 minutes (if the mixture looks too dry add the extra ½ cup liquid) or the rice is just cooked through with no hard centres, add the frozen peas or beans and season to taste with salt and pepper. (The sausage tends to be fairly salty so you probably won't need extra salt.)

Cook for about 2 minutes longer, then pile onto serving plates and garnish with some shaved or grated parmesan. Serve with crusty bread or bruschetta and a green salad.

Chicken, tomato and basil risotto

Creamy chicken and mushroom risotto

This is another variation on my 'instant-meal' theme. I usually have mushrooms in the fridge, so I can pull a small package of boneless skinless chicken out of the freezer, thaw it in the microwave and put this risotto together in about 40 minutes all up – without any forethought or planning.

For 2–3 servings:

2 tablespoons olive oil
1 medium onion, diced
2 cloves garlic, crushed, peeled and chopped
250–300g boneless skinless chicken, cubed
1 red chilli, deseeded and chopped (or ½ teaspoon minced red chilli), (optional)
250g mushrooms, sliced
½ red capsicum, deseeded and diced
½ teaspoon thyme
1 cup arborio (or calrose) rice
2½ cups boiling water
2 teaspoons instant mushroom stock
¼ cup cream
¼ cup grated parmesan cheese
salt and pepper to taste
basil or thyme and a little additional parmesan cheese to garnish

Heat the oil in a large, preferably non-stick, pan. Add the onion and garlic to the pan and cook, stirring frequently, until the onion is soft (about 2 minutes). Add the chicken and chilli (if using) to the pan and continue to cook until the chicken is no longer pink.

Stir in the mushrooms, capsicum and thyme and cook, stirring occasionally, until the mushrooms have softened. Add the rice and cook for 2–3 minutes longer, stirring constantly.

Add 1 cup of the water and the instant stock powder. Bring to the boil, then reduce the heat to a gentle simmer and cook, stirring frequently, until the liquid has almost disappeared. Add the remaining water ½ cup at a time and simmer, stirring frequently, until the liquid has almost gone before making the next addition.

When all the water has been added (and absorbed) and the risotto has cooked for about 20 minutes, test to see if the rice is cooked through – it should be firm but with no hard centres. (If necessary, add another ¼ – ½ cup water and simmer for a few minutes longer.) When the rice is cooked, add the cream and parmesan and stir to mix. Season to taste with salt and pepper.

Heat through, then serve immediately, garnished with a little basil or thyme and some shaved or grated parmesan (if you want). As with most risottos, a crisp green salad, some crusty bread and a glass of wine make ideal accompaniments.

Pumpkin, bacon and mushroom risotto

The pumpkin gives this risotto a lovely warm glow, while the bacon and mushrooms provide 'depth' and delicious, slightly earthy flavours.

If you want to make a vegetarian version, simply omit the bacon – the result is still extremely good and satisfying.

For 3–4 large servings:

1 tablespoon olive (or canola) oil
1 medium onion, quartered and sliced
1–2 cloves garlic, crushed, peeled and chopped
150–200g bacon, cut in 1cm ribbons
1 cup arborio (or calrose) rice
2 tablespoons olive (or canola) oil
250g seeded and peeled pumpkin, grated
250g white or brown button mushrooms, sliced
2½–3 cups hot water
2–3 teaspoons instant mushroom stock
1 tablespoon pesto
2–3 tablespoons grated parmesan cheese
½ –1 cup fresh or frozen peas
salt and pepper to taste

Heat the first measure of oil in a large, preferably non-stick, frypan. Add the onion, garlic and bacon then cook, stirring frequently, until the onion is soft and clear and the bacon is golden, about 5 minutes, then stir in the rice and cook for 1–2 minutes longer. Remove the rice mixture from the pan and set aside.

Heat the second measure of oil in the pan and add the pumpkin and mushrooms. Cook, stirring frequently to avoid browning, for about 5 minutes.

Return the rice mixture to the pan and stir gently, then add 1 cup of the water and the instant stock powder. Bring to the boil, then reduce the heat to a gentle simmer, stirring occasionally, until most of the liquid has disappeared (3–4 minutes). Add another cup of liquid and when this has been absorbed, add another ½ cup of liquid and leave to simmer again.

When this liquid has almost gone, begin testing the rice to see if it is cooked through – if the risotto looks too dry before the rice is cooked, add an extra ½ cup or so of water and cook a little longer. Don't overcook or the rice will turn a bit mushy, but don't serve it undercooked either – hard-centred rice is very unpleasant!

As soon as the grains are tender right through, add the pesto, parmesan and peas, then cook, stirring frequently, until the peas are cooked, another 3–4 minutes. Season to taste with salt and pepper (you may not need any salt if you used instant stock or the bacon was salty).

Serve immediately, topped with some chopped basil and/or shaved or grated parmesan.

the rice doesn't catch on the bottom. If the mixture looks too dry during this time, add another ¼ cup water (repeat if necessary).

When the rice is cooked, stir in the beans and coriander and add salt to taste. Serve as is, topping each serving with a dollop of sour cream and a little extra chopped fresh coriander, or, use as a filling for enchiladas or burritos (see the recipes in Burgers, Kebabs & Wraps on page 44).

Mexican rice and beans

I don't know about its actual authenticity, but this simple and delicious one-pot bean and rice mixture certainly tastes the part! Serve it as is, or use it to fill flour tortillas to make burritos or enchiladas.

For 4 servings:
2 tablespoons olive (or canola) oil
1 medium onion, diced
1–2 cloves garlic, peeled and chopped
1 large green capsicum, deseeded and diced
1 cup long grain rice
1 teaspoon each ground cumin and oregano
½ teaspoon chilli powder
300g can tomato purée
1½–2 cups hot water
425g can red kidney beans, drained
2 tablespoons chopped fresh coriander
½ –1 teaspoon salt
sour cream and chopped fresh coriander to garnish

Heat the oil in a large (lidded) pan. Add the onion and garlic and sauté until the onion is soft. Stir in the capsicum and cook, stirring frequently, for 1–2 minutes longer.

Add the rice and stir until it is evenly coated with oil. Cook, stirring frequently, until the rice has turned milky white, then add the cumin, oregano, chilli powder and tomato purée. Pour in 1½ cups hot water and stir until everything is well combined. Bring the mixture to the boil, then reduce the heat to a gentle simmer and cover. Cook for about 15 minutes or until the rice is just tender, stirring occasionally to make sure

Chicken and rice chilli

This delicious Tex-Mex rice mixture can be served as a meal on its own, but it also makes a great all-in-one filling for burritos, tacos etc.

If you don't have 2 cups of leftover cooked rice on hand, don't worry – as soon as you start thinking about making this, cover 1 cup long grain rice with 2 cups boiling water and microwave at 50% power for 15–17 minutes in a covered container. (If you don't have a microwave sprinkle 1 cup long grain rice into a large pot of boiling water and boil, stirring occasionally, for 8–10 minutes or until the rice is cooked through, then drain it well.)

For 4 servings:
2 tablespoons olive (or canola) oil
1 medium onion, diced
500g boneless skinless chicken, cubed or sliced
2 teaspoons cumin
1 teaspoon oregano
½ teaspoon chilli powder
1 red capsicum, deseeded and diced
1 green capsicum, deseeded and diced
2 sticks celery, sliced
400g can whole tomatoes in juice
2 cups cooked rice (see above)
310g can kidney beans
½ –1 teaspoon salt
3–4 tablespoons chopped coriander

Heat the oil in a large non-stick pan, then add the onion and cook, stirring occasionally, for about 2 minutes until the onion has softened. Add the chicken and continue to cook, stirring frequently, until the chicken is no longer pink.

Stir in the cumin, oregano and chilli powder and cook for about a minute longer, then add the capsicums and celery. Cook, stirring every now and then, for about 5 minutes, or until the chicken is cooked through (to test, cut through a thick piece to see that there is no pink in the middle).

Drain the tomatoes, reserving the juice, and dice the flesh. Add the tomatoes (plus juice), the rice and the rinsed and drained beans to the pan and stir to combine. Allow the chilli mixture to heat through, then season to taste with salt and add the chopped coriander.

Serve as is, accompanied with a diced avocado (or other green) salad, or accompany with bowls of shredded lettuce, diced tomato, grated cheese and a little sour cream to use as fillings in soft corn or flour tortillas for an 'assemble-your-own' dinner.

Spicy gumbo

Gumbo, by definition, is a mixture of different foods and flavours. I think this version is delicious, but there are few hard and fast rules, so feel free to make substitutions or additions...

For 3–4 servings:
2 tablespoons canola oil
1 medium onion, diced
2 cloves garlic, peeled and chopped
100g ham, diced
2 (about 100g) spicy sausages (chorizo etc), sliced
1 medium red capsicum, deseeded and diced
2–3 sticks celery, sliced
1 teaspoon paprika
½ teaspoon each cayenne pepper, ground black
    pepper and thyme
2 bay leaves
400g can whole tomatoes in juice
1 cup chicken stock (or water or white wine)
1 cup corn kernels, frozen, canned or fresh
2 cups cooked rice
1–2 cups cooked peeled shrimp, fresh or frozen
    (optional)
salt to taste
2–3 tablespoons chopped parsley

Heat the oil in a large, preferably non-stick, pan or pot. Add the onion and garlic to the pan and cook, stirring frequently, until the onion is soft. Stir in the diced ham and sliced sausages and cook for about 3 minutes.

Add the capsicum and celery to the pan along with the spices, thyme and bay leaves. Cook, stirring continuously, for another 2–3 minutes, then add the tomatoes in their juice (break up the whole tomatoes), and the stock (or water or wine).

Bring the mixture to the boil and stir in the corn and cooked rice. Simmer until the corn is cooked, then add the shrimp (if using) and heat through.

Season to taste with salt (if required) then add the chopped parsley. Serve accompanied with crusty bread and/or a salad.

Kedgeree

Kedgeree is another dish that exists in many forms. It can be made with smoked or plain fish and with or without the curry powder, but I think the addition of both makes it more interesting!

I don't know how I feel about kedgeree for breakfast, as it was served in the days of the Raj, but I do think it makes a great lunch or dinner.

For 3–4 servings:
1½ cups basmati (or long grain) rice
400g smoked fish, skinned and boned
1 cup hot water
2–3 bay leaves
1 teaspoon whole peppercorns
1 tablespoon canola oil
2 tablespoons butter
2 medium onions, quartered and sliced
2 cloves garlic, crushed, peeled and chopped
1 red capsicum, deseeded and diced
1 tablespoon curry powder
½ –1 cup frozen peas
½ –1 teaspoon salt
2–3 tablespoons chopped coriander, parsley or spring onion

Cook the rice according to the instructions in Chicken and Rice Chilli on the page opposite.

While the rice cooks, place the fish in a large frypan and add the water, bay leaves and peppercorns, then simmer for 3–5 minutes until the fish is soft. Transfer the fish to a bowl and break up into bite-sized flakes or pieces (keep an eye out for any small bones that you missed the first time round). Strain and reserve the liquid.

Heat the oil and butter together in the pan, then add the onions and garlic and cook, stirring occasionally, until the onions are soft. Stir in the capsicum and continue to cook until the onions are just beginning to brown. Sprinkle in the curry powder and stir-fry for 1 minute, then add the cooked rice, flaked fish and peas to the pan. Stir to combine, adding enough of the reserved liquid to moisten the mixture.

Heat gently for 3–5 minutes, adding extra liquid if required, then season to taste with salt. Stir in the fresh herbs then serve.

Chicken biryani

When I first attempted making biryani I was trying to emulate the dish I had in one of my favourite Indian restaurants. However, as I looked around for recipes I found that many different styles and even methods were used to make these rice and meat dishes.

My version turned out to be quite different from the restaurant version, but is still delicious...

For 2–3 large servings:
1½ cups basmati rice
¼ teaspoon saffron threads soaked in 1 tablespoon boiling water (optional)
10cm cinnamon stick
4 green cardamom pods
1½ cups boiling water
2 tablespoons canola oil
1 medium onion, diced
2 cloves garlic, crushed, peeled and chopped
2–3cm root ginger, grated or chopped
300–400g boneless skinless chicken
3 tablespoons curry paste
3 tomatoes, chopped or diced
1 teaspoon salt
1 cup peas
1–2 tablespoons each currants and sliced almonds

Rinse the rice with plenty of water, then cover with fresh water and leave to soak for about 20–30 minutes.

Drain soaked rice, then add the soaked saffron and water (if using), cinnamon stick and cardamom pods. Add the boiling water then cover and microwave at medium (50%) power for 15 minutes (you can do this in advance if you want).

Heat the oil in a large non-stick pan, add the onion and cook, stirring frequently, for about 3 minutes or until the onion has softened. Add the garlic and the ginger. Cook for 3–5 minutes longer, stirring occasionally, until the mixture begins to brown.

Add the chicken and stir-fry until no longer pink, then add curry paste. Cook, stirring frequently, for 1–2 minutes longer, then add the tomatoes and salt. Stir-fry for another 2–3 minutes, then remove from the heat and mix in the peas.

Spread half the rice over the bottom of a lightly oiled or non-stick sprayed 20 x 30cm casserole dish, arrange the chicken mixture over the rice, then spread the remaining rice over this.

Sprinkle the top with currants and sliced almonds, then cover with foil and bake at 180°C for 15–20 minutes. Serve accompanied with naan or other Indian breads and a selection of chutneys.

Pasta with spicy eggplant and chorizo sauce

Pasta makes an ideal basis for no-fuss summer meals. The combination of eggplant, tomatoes and basil in this sauce really says summer while the spicy chorizo (Spanish sausage) gives it a little more 'bite' and substance.

Chorizos are available from the deli counter of most supermarkets (or delicatessens or specialty butchers), but don't worry if you can't find them – the same weight of a good spicy salami or even bierstick will give a similar result.

I have suggested stirring this thick, chunky sauce through rigatoni (short, wide pasta tubes), but of course you can serve it with almost any shape of pasta that you have on hand.

For 3–4 servings:
2–3 tablespoons olive oil
1 medium (about 350g) eggplant, cut into 1–2cm cubes
1 tablespoon olive oil
1 medium onion, diced
2–3 cloves garlic, peeled and chopped
2 chorizos (150–200g in total)
400g can whole tomatoes in juice
1 tablespoon balsamic vinegar (or 1–2 teaspoons wine vinegar)
300–350g rigatoni (or other pasta)
½–1 teaspoon salt
black pepper to taste
3–4 tablespoons chopped fresh basil
shaved or grated parmesan to garnish

Heat 2 tablespoons oil in a large, preferably non-stick, pan. Add the eggplant to the pan and cook, stirring frequently, for about 5 minutes until the eggplant has softened and is lightly browned. If the eggplant soaks up all the oil and begins to look too dry, add the extra tablespoon of oil. Remove eggplant from the pan and set aside.

Heat the second measure of oil in the pan then add the onion and garlic and cook, stirring occasionally, until the onion has softened. Quarter the chorizos lengthwise, then slice into pieces 5–10mm thick. Stir these into the onion and cook, turning every now and then, for about 5 minutes.

Tip the tomatoes and juice into the pan, breaking up the whole tomatoes with a fish slice or spoon. Add the vinegar and the eggplant cubes. Stir to mix, then reduce the heat and leave to simmer gently while you cook the pasta according to the instructions on the packet.

Drain the cooked pasta and return it to the cooking pot. Gently stir the sauce through the pasta, then season to taste with salt and pepper, and add the fresh basil (reserve a little to use as a garnish).

Transfer the pasta to a serving platter or individual plates and top with some shaved or grated fresh parmesan and garnish with the reserved basil.

Serve immediately accompanied with some crusty bread and a crisp green salad.

Seafood medley with creamy coriander and lime sauce

Quick, elegant and delicious – seafood served in this velvety crème fraîche sauce is hard to beat!

On closer examination of this recipe, you will notice that there are no vegetables in it, so it really should be accompanied with a side dish of salad or some lightly cooked seasonal vegetables.

For 2–3 servings:
200–300g fresh pasta
about 1 tablespoon olive oil
1 cup dry white wine
2 cloves garlic, crushed
½ teaspoon black peppercorns
1–2 bay leaves
1 teaspoon Dijon mustard
500g assorted seafood (firm white fish, calamari,
     shellfish, prawns etc.)
finely grated rind and juice of 1 lime
200–250g crème fraîche
½ –1 teaspoon salt
2 tablespoons chopped fresh coriander

Cook the pasta in plenty of boiling water, drain, then return it to the cooking pot, toss with the olive oil and set aside.

Combine the wine, garlic, peppercorns, bay leaves and mustard in a large pan. Bring mixture to the boil, then add the seafood and poach until barely cooked (about 3–5 minutes).

Remove and set aside the seafood, then strain the cooking liquid into another container. Return the liquid to the pan, bring to the boil over a high heat and reduce down to about a third of its original volume. Stir in the finely grated lime rind and juice and crème fraîche. Bring to the boil then reduce the heat to a gentle simmer. Season to taste with salt, then gently stir the cooked seafood and chopped coriander into the sauce.

Arrange pasta on warmed serving plates, top with the seafood then spoon over any remaining sauce. Serve immediately, adding a crisp green salad or steamed vegetables and a glass of your favourite wine for a really elegant meal.

Quick spaghetti bolognese

This type of meat sauce may not bear much resemblance to the original Italian version from which it takes its name, but it is good, quick and versatile.

You can serve this any number of different ways; divide the pasta between individual plates and top with sauce, arrange the pasta on a serving platter and top with sauce, or, toss sauce through the cooked pasta and arrange on a serving platter. Whichever way you choose it's good garnished with some shaved or grated parmesan cheese, chopped parsley and/or some shredded basil.

For 4–6 servings:
2 tablespoons olive oil
1 medium onion, diced
2 cloves garlic, crushed, peeled and chopped
½ red or green capsicum, diced (optional)
2 medium carrots, finely diced
2 sticks celery, thinly sliced
400g lean minced beef
½ teaspoon each dried basil and marjoram
2 x 400g cans whole tomatoes in juice
3–4 tablespoons tomato paste
salt and pepper to taste
400–500g long pasta (spaghetti, fettuccine etc.)
freshly shaved or grated parmesan cheese and/or
     chopped parsley or basil to garnish

Heat the oil in a large pan, then add the onion and garlic. Cook until the onion has softened then add the prepared vegetables and cook for 2 minutes longer. Add the minced beef and cook until lightly browned, stirring frequently to break up any large lumps.

Stir in the dried herbs then add the tomatoes and tomato paste. Crush or mash the whole tomatoes with the back of a spoon.

Bring the mixture to the boil, stirring occasionally. Reduce the heat and leave the uncovered sauce to simmer gently while you cook the pasta. Season to taste with salt and pepper.

When the pasta is cooked, drain briefly, then toss with a little extra olive oil. Top the pasta with the sauce (see introduction), garnish, and serve immediately. As with most pasta dishes, a salad and/or bread make ideal accompaniments.

Seafood medley with creamy coriander and lime sauce

Pastitio

Pastitio is a delicious Greek dish, similar in some ways to lasagne. Like most lasagnes, while it arrives at the table in one dish, it is actually assembled in several different steps. I have simplified this version as much as I can, and think that the effort required during assembly is well worth the result on the table.

For 4–6 servings:

250g long pasta (ziti, mafalda or lasagne ribbons etc.)
2 tablespoons olive oil
1 medium onion, diced
2–3 cloves garlic, crushed, peeled and chopped
500g lean minced lamb or beef
½ cup water
1 teaspoon instant beef or vegetable stock (or wine)
370g jar (1½ cups) prepared pasta sauce
1–2 teaspoons oregano
salt and pepper to taste
250g ricotta (or cottage) cheese
½ teaspoon salt
¼ teaspoon grated nutmeg (optional)
2 cups plain unsweetened yoghurt
2 large eggs
1 cup grated tasty cheese

Cook the pasta in plenty of boiling water, and preheat the oven to 200°C.

While the pasta cooks prepare the meat sauce. Heat the oil in a large pan, add the onion and garlic and cook over a high heat for about 2 minutes, stirring frequently.

Add the mince, stir to break up any lumps and cook until it has lost its pink colour. Pour in the water, stock and pasta sauce. Allow to simmer for about 5 minutes then remove from the heat and add the oregano and salt and pepper to taste.

Drain the cooked pasta, then stir in the ricotta or cottage cheese, second measure of salt and the grated nutmeg (if using). Press the pasta mixture into the bottom of a lightly oiled or non-stick sprayed casserole dish (20 x 30cm). Spread the meat sauce over the pasta mixture.

Prepare the topping by whisking together the yoghurt and eggs, pour this mixture over the mince, then sprinkle with the grated cheese. Bake at 200°C for 15–20 minutes, or until the topping is set and has turned golden brown.

Leave to stand for a few minutes, then serve with some seasonal green vegetables, or a green salad and bread.

Mushroom lasagne

If you like mushrooms, you'll love this easy lasagne. It makes a great 'everyday' meal, but it's also ideal for entertaining, especially if you are cooking for a group that includes vegetarians.

For 4–6 servings:

2 tablespoons olive (or canola) oil
1 large onion, quartered and sliced
2 cloves garlic, crushed, peeled and chopped
500g mushrooms, cut into 1cm slices
1 tablespoon basil pesto
½ teaspoon salt
black pepper to taste
2–3 tablespoons (25g) butter
3 tablespoons flour
about ¼ teaspoon freshly grated nutmeg
½ teaspoon salt
2½ cups milk
1 cup grated tasty cheese
150–200g fresh lasagne sheets

Heat the oil in a large, preferably lidded, non-stick pan. Add the onion and garlic and cook, stirring frequently, until the onion is soft and clear. Gently stir in the mushrooms, then cover the pan and cook, stirring occasionally, until they have softened and wilted. Remove from the heat and add the pesto and salt and pepper to taste.

Melt the butter in a medium pot. Stir in the flour and cook, stirring continuously, for 1 minute. Add the nutmeg and salt then 1 cup of the milk. Stir well to ensure there are no lumps and allow the sauce to thicken and boil, then add the remaining milk and bring to the boil again, stirring frequently. Remove from the heat and stir in the grated cheese.

Preheat the oven to 200°C. Lightly oil or non-stick spray a 20 x 25cm casserole dish. Spread ½ cup cheese sauce over the bottom of the dish, then cover this with a sheet of lasagne. Cover this with half of the mushroom mixture, ½ cup cheese sauce, then another sheet of lasagne. Repeat the layering process, finishing with another sheet of lasagne.

Spread the remaining cheese sauce over the top, then bake the lasagne for 30–40 minutes, until the top is golden brown. Remove from the oven and leave to stand for 5 minutes before serving.

Note:

Lasagne can be made ahead and reheated covered (about 30 minutes, or until the centre is warm, at 175°C) when required.

Baked vegetable and macaroni cheese

I have always loved macaroni cheese! I'm happy to eat it served straight from the pot, but my father insists that to be a meal it must be topped with crumbs and baked the way his grandmother used to make it. I will concede that baked macaroni cheese is especially good, so here's a variation on the theme.

For 4 large servings:

250g short pasta (macaroni, spirals, curls etc.)
200g broccoli, cut into small florets
425g can whole tomatoes in juice
25g butter
3 tablespoons flour
1 cup milk
½ –1 teaspoon salt
black pepper to taste
½ teaspoon basil or marjoram
1 cup grated tasty cheese
2 slices bread
1 clove garlic, peeled
1 tablespoon olive or canola oil

Bring a large pot of water to the boil, then add the pasta. When the pasta is almost cooked (after 8–10 minutes boiling) add the broccoli florets and cook for a further 2–3 minutes. When the pasta is cooked, drain the pasta-broccoli mixture then transfer it to a lightly oiled or non-stick sprayed 25 x 30cm casserole dish. Preheat the oven to 225°C.

Drain the tomatoes, reserving the juice, and roughly chop the flesh, then add this to the pasta mixture. Melt the butter in the pot you used to cook the pasta, stir in the flour and cook, stirring continuously, for about a minute. Add half the milk and stir until the mixture thickens and boils, ensuring there are no lumps. Add the remaining milk and reserved tomato juice and allow the sauce to thicken and boil again. Remove the sauce from the heat then add salt and pepper to taste, the basil or marjoram and the grated cheese. Stir until the cheese has melted.

Place the bread and garlic in a blender or food processor, process until bread is crumbed, then add the oil and process again.

Pour the sauce over the pasta and vegetable mixture, and stir to combine. Sprinkle with the crumb mixture, then bake at 225°C for 15–20 minutes or until the top begins to brown.

Serve alone or with a salad and/or crusty bread.

Mince and mushroom dinner

This is an updated version of a very popular comfort food from my childhood – the addition of some extra vegetables has enhanced its ability to stand up as a one-dish meal without affecting its appeal for children.

For 3–4 servings:

2 tablespoons olive (or canola) oil
1 medium onion, diced
1 large clove garlic, crushed, peeled and chopped
200g mushrooms, sliced
400–500g minced beef
1 medium carrot, finely diced
½ teaspoon each dried thyme and tarragon
425g can condensed mushroom soup
1½ cups boiling water
½ cup white wine (or additional ½ cup boiling water)
125g small pasta shapes (spirals are good)
1 cup frozen peas
1 tablespoon Worcestershire sauce
¼ cup regular or lite sour cream
salt and pepper, to taste
chopped parsley to serve

Heat 1 tablespoon oil in a large, lidded pot or frypan, then add the onion and garlic and cook, stirring frequently, until the onion is soft and turning clear. Add the second tablespoon of oil and the mushrooms, continue to cook, stirring occasionally, until the mushrooms have wilted.

Add the mince, carrot, thyme and tarragon to the pan and cook, breaking up any large lumps of mince, until the mince is has lost its pink colour. Stir in the soup, water and wine (if using), bring to the boil then add the pasta shapes. Return to the boil, then reduce the heat and simmer for about 10 minutes or until the pasta is just cooked (if the mixture looks too dry during this time add ¼ – ½ cup extra water). Mix in the peas and simmer for another 3–4 minutes.

Stir in the Worcestershire sauce and sour cream. Taste and season with salt and pepper if required (the soup tends to be fairly salty, so it may not need any extra).

Garnish with parsley and serve as is or accompanied with a salad or steamed vegetables.

Salmon and mushroom cannelloni

This has to be my favourite way to use canned salmon – I still find it amazing that you can turn a can of salmon into something so elegant and delicious.

By keeping a large can of salmon and some cannelloni tubes on hand in your pantry you can impress friends or family at relatively short notice.

For 4–6 servings:

2 tablespoons olive oil
1 medium onion, diced
1 clove garlic, crushed, peeled and chopped
200g small button mushrooms, sliced
415g can pink salmon
½ cup ricotta (or cottage) cheese
2 tablespoons capers (optional)
2–3 tablespoons chopped parsley
1 tablespoon chopped fresh dill (or ½ –1 teaspoon dried dill)
2–3 tablespoons (25g) butter
¼ cup flour
2½ cups milk
salt and pepper to taste
¼ teaspoon freshly grated nutmeg
2 cups grated cheese
16–20 (about 200g) cannelloni tubes
paprika to dust

Heat the oil in a large pan. Add the onion and garlic and cook for about 2 minutes, stirring frequently. Stir in the sliced mushrooms (remember the filling has to be stuffed in tubes so if the mushrooms are too large you may need to halve the slices) and cook for another 2 minutes, then remove from the heat.

Open and drain the salmon, and add this along with the ricotta (or cottage cheese) and the capers, parsley and dill. Stir until the filling ingredients are well combined, removing any obvious salmon bones. Set the filling aside to cool while you prepare the sauce.

Melt the butter in a medium pot. Add the flour and stir well so there are no lumps. Cook, stirring continuously, for about 1 minute. Pour in one third of the milk and bring to the boil, stirring vigorously, to ensure there are no lumps. Allow the sauce to thicken and boil for a minute, then add half the remaining milk and bring to the boil again, stirring frequently. Repeat, using the last of the milk, then remove the sauce from the heat. Add the seasonings and 1 cup grated cheese. Stir until the cheese melts.

Preheat the oven to 200°C. Pour a third of the cheese sauce into an oiled casserole dish. (Check to see that it will hold the cannelloni in a single layer before you start.) Stuff the filling into the cannelloni tubes using clean hands – there is no tidy way to do this! Arrange the filled cannelloni tubes in the dish. Cover with the remaining sauce, then sprinkle with the rest of the grated cheese and sprinkle the top with a few pinches of paprika.

Bake at 200°C for 30–40 minutes. Serve with crusty bread, a green or tomato salad, or steamed seasonal vegetables.

Spinach and mushroom lasagne

I have been making variations of this recipe since my early student days. It remains popular, and as far as lasagne goes, is relatively straightforward.

For 4–6 servings:

2 tablespoons olive oil
1 medium onion, diced
2 cloves garlic, crushed, peeled and chopped
250g mushrooms, sliced
½ teaspoon each dried thyme and marjoram
500g frozen spinach, thawed (or 2 cups cooked fresh spinach)
1 cup cottage cheese
½ teaspoon salt
2–3 tablespoons (25g) butter
¼ cup flour
2 cups milk
salt and pepper to taste
¼ teaspoon freshly grated nutmeg
1 cup grated cheese
250–300g curly lasagne noodles or sheets
¼ cup freshly grated parmesan cheese
paprika

Heat the olive oil in a large pan. Add the onion and garlic and cook until the onion is soft and turning clear, then add the mushrooms, thyme and marjoram. Continue to cook for 2–3 minutes longer, or until the mushrooms have wilted. Remove the pan from the heat and set aside.

Combine the spinach, cottage cheese and salt in another bowl.

Melt the butter in a medium pot. Add the flour and stir well so there are no lumps. Cook, stirring continuously for about a minute. Pour in one third of the milk and bring to the boil, stirring vigorously to ensure there are no lumps. Allow the sauce to thicken and boil for a minute, then add half the remaining milk and bring to the boil again, stirring frequently. Add the remaining milk and bring to the boil once again, then remove the sauce from the heat. Add the seasonings and 1 cup grated cheese. Stir until the cheese melts.

Preheat the oven to 180°C. Lightly oil (or non-stick spray) a 20 x 30cm casserole or lasagne dish. Cover the bottom with a single layer of lasagne. Spread half the spinach mixture evenly over the lasagne. Arrange another layer of lasagne over the spinach, then cover this with the mushroom mixture. Add another layer of lasagne, then the remaining spinach mixture and a final layer of lasagne. Pour the cheese sauce over the top and sprinkle this with the grated parmesan.

Dust the top lightly with paprika and bake at 180°C for 40–45 minutes. Serve with bread and/or a side salad.

Variation:

If you combine the spinach and mushroom mixtures, they make a great filling for cannelloni. Simply use the mixture to fill cannelloni tubes, following the instructions in Salmon and Mushroom Cannelloni on page 66. If you don't want to make a cheese sauce, you can use a 500g jar of bought tomato pasta sauce instead, sprinkle the top with 2 cups of grated cheese, then bake as above.

Beef lasagne

I think it's quite fascinating how food 'fashions' change – 20 years ago lasagne was probably viewed as something foreign and exotic, now to many people, myself included, it has reached 'comfort food' status.

Making lasagne from start to finish does take a while, but all of the individual stages are actually very simple. Better still, if you know you are going to be short of time, it can be prepared ahead and reheated when required.

For 4–6 servings:
2 tablespoons olive oil
1 large onion, diced
2 cloves garlic, chopped
500g minced beef
300g can tomato purée
425g can Italian seasoned tomatoes
1 teaspoon salt
½ teaspoon sugar

1 tablespoon pesto (or 1 teaspoon basil)
25g butter
3 tablespoons flour
2 cups milk
225–250g lasagne sheets or noodles
1½ cups grated cheese
½ teaspoon salt
grated nutmeg and pepper to taste
paprika for dusting

Heat the oil in a large frypan and lightly brown the onion and garlic. Add the minced beef and cook, stirring frequently, until the mince has lost its pink colour and begins to brown.

Stir in the tomato purée, seasoned tomatoes, salt, sugar and pesto (or basil). Allow the mixture to boil, then lower the heat and leave to simmer gently while you prepare the cheese sauce.

Melt the butter in a medium pot. Add the flour and stir well to ensure there are no lumps. Cook, stirring continuously, for 1 minute. Pour in half the milk and bring to the boil, stirring frequently. Add the remaining milk and bring to the boil again, stirring frequently, then remove from the heat and stir in the second measure of salt and a cup of the grated cheese.

Preheat the oven to 180°C. Spread a third of the mince mixture in the bottom of a lightly oiled 20 x 30cm casserole dish. Arrange a third of the noodles in a single layer over the mince, then spread half of the remaining mince mixture over this. Add another layer of pasta, then repeat this process with the remaining mince and noodles, so you have three layers of each, finishing with pasta. Pour the cheese sauce over the pasta, and spread evenly so the entire surface is covered. Sprinkle with the remaining grated cheese and dust lightly with paprika.

Bake for 30–45 minutes at 180°C then leave to stand for 10–15 minutes before cutting. Serve with bread and a crisp green salad.

Note:

Don't assemble lasagne and leave to sit uncooked, the pasta will turn soggy – bake it first and reheat when required.

Easy smoked salmon and mushroom lasagne

This recipe is so simple to make and has been so popular whenever I've served it that I thought it justified inclusion in this book, even if it really does need to be served with a salad or vegetables alongside.

For 4 servings:
2–3 tablespoons (25g) butter
3 tablespoons flour
½ teaspoon salt
black pepper to taste
¼ teaspoon grated nutmeg
2½ cups milk
2 cups grated cheese
200g button mushrooms, sliced
150–200g smoked salmon, sliced
100–200g fresh lasagne sheets
paprika to dust

Melt the butter in a large pot. Add the flour and stir to form a thick paste. Continue to cook, stirring frequently, for 1–2 minutes. Add the salt, pepper and nutmeg, stir, then add about a third of the milk.

Whisk or stir vigorously until the mixture thickens and boils and ensure that there are no lumps. Cook for 1–2 minutes, stirring frequently, then add another third of the milk, stirring until the mixture boils again. Add the remaining milk, and bring to the boil for the last time.

Remove the sauce from the heat and stir in about three-quarters of the grated cheese.

Preheat the oven to 180°C, then lightly oil or non-stick spray a shallow casserole or lasagne dish. Spread ½ cup of the sauce over the bottom of the dish, then cover with a sheet of lasagne. Arrange about half of the sliced mushrooms and half the smoked salmon over the lasagne then cover these with about a third of the remaining sauce. Cover with another sheet lasagne. Make another layer with the remaining mushroom and salmon, then cover with half the remaining sauce. Cover this with another layer of lasagne then pour in the remaining sauce and spread so the whole surface is covered.

Sprinkle the top with the rest of the grated cheese and a little paprika. Bake for 30–40 minutes at 180°C or until the top is golden brown. Serve with a green or tomato salad, or steamed seasonal vegetables and crusty or garlic bread.

Creamy mushroom stroganoff

Button mushrooms in this delicious creamy sauce served over pasta (or rice) make a wonderful quick meal.

For 3–4 servings:
300–400g long pasta (fettuccine, spaghetti etc.)
2 tablespoons olive oil
1 medium onion, quartered and sliced
500g button mushrooms, halved
½ teaspoon tarragon
¼ teaspoon thyme
¼ cup sherry (or dry red or white wine)
1 tablespoon each tomato paste and dark soy sauce
250g regular or lite sour cream
2–3 tablespoons chopped parsley
½ –1 teaspoon salt
freshly ground black pepper to taste
chopped parsley and paprika to garnish

Put the pasta on to cook in plenty of rapidly boiling water. While the pasta cooks prepare the sauce.

Heat the olive oil in a large pan, add the sliced onion and cook, stirring frequently, until the onion begins to brown. Add the halved mushrooms and continue to cook, stirring occasionally, until the mushrooms have softened and wilted.

Gently stir in the tarragon, thyme, sherry (or wine), tomato paste and soy sauce. Leave the sauce to simmer for 3–5 minutes then stir in the sour cream. Reheat without boiling, then add the chopped parsley and season to taste with salt and pepper.

Spoon stroganoff over the drained and lightly oiled pasta, garnish with some additional chopped parsley and a dash of paprika. Serve immediately, accompanied with steamed vegetables or a salad.

Easy smoked salmon and mushroom lasagne

Fish Veracruz

I don't know if this simple Mexican dish really qualifies as a curry (or stir-fry), but it is so quick and easy to prepare it seems a pity to have to classify it with the casseroles. A couple of dried chillies and a hint of coriander really do give this a delicious, spicy flavour.

The dried red chillies I use for this are 5–7.5cm long (I usually get them in Asian food stores) and give a pleasant 'heat' rather than fiery 'hotness' that seems to come from their tiny and more widely available cousins.

For 3–4 servings:
2 tablespoons olive oil
1 medium onion, quartered and sliced
2–3 cloves garlic, crushed, peeled and chopped
2 dried red chillies, deseeded and sliced
1 green capsicum, deseeded, quartered and sliced
2 bay leaves
1 teaspoon cumin
½ teaspoon oregano
400g can whole tomatoes in juice
500g firm-fleshed fish fillets (snapper, monkfish,
    warehou etc.), cubed
1–2 tablespoons chopped fresh coriander
1 tablespoon lime (or lemon) juice
about ½ teaspoon salt

Heat the oil in a large frypan. Add the onion and garlic and cook until the onion softens, then add the chillies, green capsicum and the bay leaves.

Continue to cook, stirring occasionally, until the onion is translucent and the green capsicum is soft, then add the cumin and oregano. Drain the tomatoes reserving the juice, then crush the whole tomatoes and add them to the pan with about half the juice.

Gently stir in the cubed fish and simmer gently for about 5 minutes, stirring once or twice to turn the fish (add the remaining tomato liquid if the mixture begins to look dry). Remove from the heat as soon as the largest cubes of fish are just cooked, and stir in the coriander, lime (or lemon) juice and salt to taste.

Serve immediately over plainly cooked rice. A crisp green salad and a cold beer make ideal accompaniments.

Fish Veracruz

Braised eggplant with pork

I first tried this dish in San Francisco as part of a 'take-out' buffet enjoyed with friends. It has taken me several attempts to come up with a version that compares favourably with the original, but I think it was well worth persevering!

For 2–3 servings:

500g (2 small) eggplant
4 tablespoons canola oil
2 large cloves garlic, peeled and chopped
½ medium onion, diced
150–200g minced pork
2 tablespoons rice wine or sherry
1 teaspoon cornflour
1 tablespoon dark soy sauce
½ cup water
1 teaspoon sesame oil
½ teaspoon instant chicken stock
¼ teaspoon sugar
¼ – ½ teaspoon salt
1–2 tablespoons chopped fresh coriander

Top and tail the eggplants and cut them lengthwise into quarters, then halve each quarter lengthwise again. Cut the wedges into pieces about 5cm long.

Heat 2 tablespoons of the oil in a large non-stick pan or wok, and add half the eggplant pieces. Cook for about 5 minutes, turning once or twice, until the cut surfaces are golden brown. Remove the first batch from the pan and set aside, then add anther tablespoon of oil and brown the remaining eggplant the same way, then remove from pan.

Heat the remaining canola oil and cook the garlic and onion, stirring frequently, until soft and beginning to brown. Add the minced pork and stir-fry until the pork looks opaque. Sprinkle in the rice wine or sherry and continue to cook until it has mostly evaporated. Mix the cornflour to a paste with the soy sauce in a small bowl, then stir in the water, sesame oil, instant stock, and sugar.

Stir the browned eggplant into the pork, then add the soy-water mixture and simmer for 5–10 minutes, stirring occasionally, until the eggplant is very tender. Season to taste with salt (if required).

Garnish with the chopped coriander and serve with steamed rice.

Chicken and vegetable curry

This easy curry is a great way to turn frozen chicken pieces into a really interesting meal. The list of ingredients may look long, but don't be put off – most of them are spices and are all added at once so it really is quite simple to prepare!

For 3–4 servings:

2 tablespoons canola or olive oil
1 tablespoon curry powder (mild or hot*)
1 teaspoon ground turmeric
4–6 whole cloves
3–4cm cinnamon stick (or ½ –1 teaspoon ground cinnamon)
1 large onion, very finely diced
1 clove of garlic, peeled and chopped
2 tablespoons finely chopped fresh ginger
500g–700g small chicken pieces (drumsticks, wings or nibbles)
3–4 small potatoes, cubed
¾ cup chicken stock (or water)
¾ cup coconut cream
1–2 cups green vegetables (frozen peas/beans/mixed vegetables, broccoli, zucchini etc.)
½ –1 teaspoon salt
1–2 tablespoons chopped fresh coriander (optional)

Heat the oil in a large (preferably non-stick) pan, add the next seven ingredients and cook, stirring frequently, until the onion is soft and beginning to turn clear.

Add the chicken pieces and continue to cook, stirring at regular intervals, until the chicken is lightly browned on all sides. Stir in the cubed potatoes, chicken stock (or water) and coconut cream. Allow the mixture to come to the boil, then reduce the heat and simmer until the potato is tender and the chicken is cooked through. If you want the sauce thin, cover the mixture and simmer it gently. For a thicker mixture, leave uncovered and simmer a little more vigorously.

Cut the vegetables into bite-sized pieces, then add these to the mixture and simmer for a few minutes longer until the vegetables are just cooked. Add salt and coriander (if using) to taste.

Serve as is, accompanied with naan bread or roti (look in the frozen food section of your supermarket), or serve over steamed rice.

*You can vary the 'hotness' by using hot or mild curry powder (most supermarkets now have both).

Curried cauliflower and eggs

I have to confess that despite my mother's best efforts, I am not a great cauliflower fan. I can, however, make an exception for this dish – it really is much more interesting and delicious than it sounds!

For 3–4 large servings:

4 large eggs
1 tablespoon canola oil
1 medium onion, quartered and sliced
2 medium-small potatoes (200g total)
    cut into 1cm cubes
2 cloves garlic, crushed, peeled and chopped
1 tablespoon finely grated ginger
1 tablespoon curry powder
2 cardamom pods, crushed (optional)
4–5 whole cloves (optional)
400g can whole tomatoes in juice
¾ cup coconut cream
250g cauliflower, cut into florets
1 teaspoon garam masala
½ cup frozen peas (optional)
1–2 tablespoons chopped fresh coriander
½ teaspoon salt

Put the eggs in a small pot and cover with hot water, bring to the boil and simmer for 12 minutes. (Making a small whole in the blunt end of each egg will help prevent them cracking or splitting.) Cover with cold water to cool, then peel and set them aside.

Heat the oil in a large pan, then add the onion, potatoes, garlic and ginger. Cook (preferably covered) without browning for 5 minutes, stirring occasionally, then add the curry powder and the whole spices (if using). Continue to cook, stirring frequently, for 1 minute longer, then add the tomatoes in their juice. Break up the tomatoes with a spoon, stir, then cover the mixture and simmer gently until the potatoes are tender, about 5–10 minutes.

Stir in the coconut cream, cauliflower florets and garam masala. Simmer uncovered for another 5 minutes, or until the cauliflower is tender.

Mix in the peas (if using), coriander and salt, cook for 1–2 minutes longer before adding the quartered or roughly chopped hard-boiled eggs.

Served alone this makes a meal for three, but can easily be 'stretched' to feed four or five adults if served on steamed rice and accompanied with Indian breads.

Chicken korma

Korma is a great way to introduce 'novices' (adults or children) to Indian food – the creamy sauce has an interesting flavour but is not at all hot. Even my young daughter really enjoys this version!

For 3–4 servings:

½ cup blanched almonds
2 cloves garlic, peeled
2–3cm piece fresh ginger, peeled
¼ cup water
2 tablespoons canola oil
350–400g boneless skinless chicken breast,
    cut into 2cm cubes
2–3 bay leaves
5 cardamom pods
5 cloves
5cm cinnamon stick
1 medium onion, diced
2 teaspoons cumin
1 teaspoon coriander
1½ cups plain unsweetened yoghurt
1 teaspoon garam masala
½ – ¾ cup cream
½ –1 teaspoon salt
2 teaspoons canola oil
3 tablespoons each currants and slivered almonds

Place the almonds, garlic, ginger and water in a blender or food processor. Blend or process until they form a smoothish paste.

Heat the oil in a large preferably non-stick pan, then add the almond paste and chicken and stir-fry until the chicken has lost its pink colour. Add the next seven ingredients and stir-fry for a minute longer.

Pour in the yoghurt and bring to the boil, then reduce the heat to a gentle simmer and cook, stirring occasionally, for about 10 minutes or until the chicken is cooked through. Stir in the garam masala, cream and add salt to taste. Reheat without boiling.

While the korma reheats, heat the second measure of oil in a small frypan. Add the currants and slivered almonds and cook for 1–2 minutes, tossing or stirring frequently until the almonds are golden and the currants have puffed up. Add half of the currants and almonds to the korma and reserve the other half to garnish.

Serve the korma over steamed basmati rice. Naan or other Indian breads and a simple salad make ideal accompaniments.

Easy curried chicken and rice

I wouldn't want to vouch for the ethnic authenticity of this recipe, but it is easy, and is a true one-pot meal. It's not absolutely necessary to add the chickpeas, but I think they add a little extra flavour and texture and look good too.

For 4–6 servings:

2 tablespoons canola oil
6 (500 –600g total) boneless skinless chicken thighs
1 large onion, diced
2–3 cloves garlic, crushed, peeled and chopped
1 medium carrot, diced
1 green capsicum, deseeded and diced
1 tablespoon curry powder (hot or mild to taste)
1 teaspoon each ground cumin and coriander
½ teaspoon turmeric
1 cup basmati (or other long-grain) rice
400g can Indian spiced tomatoes
1½ cups boiling water
310g can chickpeas, drained and rinsed (optional)
½ –1 cup frozen peas
½ –1 teaspoon salt
2–3 tablespoons chopped fresh coriander

Heat the oil in a large, heavy casserole dish. Working in two batches, cook the chicken thighs for 3–4 minutes per side, until lightly browned.

Set the browned chicken aside and add the onion and garlic to the pot. Cook, stirring frequently, until the onion is soft and is just beginning to brown. Stir in the carrot and capsicum and cook for 2–3 minutes longer. Add the curry powder and ground spices and stir-fry for about a minute longer.

Add the rice, tomato mixture, water and the browned chicken and stir to combine. Bring to the boil, then reduce the heat to a gentle simmer and cover with a close-fitting lid. Cook for 15–20 minutes, stirring every 3–4 minutes to prevent 'catching' on the bottom, until the rice is cooked through. If the mixture is too dry before the rice is cooked, add an extra ½ cup water.

When the rice is cooked add the chickpeas (if using), frozen peas and season to taste with salt. Heat gently until the peas are cooked, then stir in the coriander.

Serve alone (for four) or if serving six add a selection of breads and/or chutneys and relishes.

Country captain chicken

This dish has an interesting history. Apparently it originated in India in the days of the Raj as an anglicised curry, but since then it has also become very popular in the USA and is now sometimes claimed as an American 'classic'.

For 6–8 servings:

2 tablespoons canola oil
1.5kg chicken portions
1 tablespoon canola oil
2 large onions, diced
4 cloves garlic, crushed, peeled and chopped
2–3cm fresh ginger, peeled and chopped
1 large green capsicum, deseeded and diced
2 tablespoons mild curry powder
½ teaspoon each cinnamon and ground cloves
400g can whole tomatoes in juice
½ cup hot water
1 teaspoon instant chicken stock
½ cup currants or sultanas
½ –1 teaspoon salt
2–3 tablespoons chopped coriander or parsley (optional)

Heat the first measure of oil in a large heavy casserole dish. Add as many chicken pieces as will fit in one layer and cook for 3–4 minutes on each side or until golden brown. Remove from the casserole and set aside, repeat until all the chicken has been browned.

Add the second measure of oil to the casserole, then add the onions, garlic and ginger and cook, stirring frequently, until the onions have softened. Stir in the capsicum and continue to cook until the onions are just beginning to brown. Measure in the curry powder and spices and cook for a minute longer, stirring constantly.

Tip in the tomatoes and juice, water and instant stock. Stir, breaking up the whole tomatoes, then add the browned chicken, arranging the pieces so they are mostly covered with the liquid. Sprinkle in the currants or sultanas.

Cover the casserole dish and simmer gently for 20–30 minutes, rearranging the chicken pieces occasionally, until the chicken is well cooked and very tender.

Season to taste with salt. Serve over steamed rice, garnished with chopped coriander or parsley (if desired), and accompanied with a salad and Indian breads.

Curried chicken noodle stir-fry

This delicious recipe originated as an attempt to emulate a favourite noodle dish of mine, bami goreng. I don't think I can claim to have recreated the original dish I was trying for, but the results were definitely good enough to be included in their own right!

You can vary the 'hotness' by using the grade (mild or hot) of curry powder that suits your taste. Beware, unless you have a very large frypan or wok, this sort of stir-fry can get messy! (I have a very large pan and the kitchen still seems to wind up looking like it's been hit by a bomb.)

Like most stir-fries, the actual cooking time is very short, but relatively full on, so it pays to prepare and/or assemble all the ingredients before you start cooking.

For 2–3 servings:
2 tablespoons canola oil
1 medium onion, cut into 12–16 thin wedges
2–3 cloves garlic, crushed, peeled and chopped
350g boneless, skinless chicken, sliced 1cm thick
1 tablespoon curry powder
1 large carrot, cut into thin matchsticks
1–2 cups small broccoli florets
2 spring onions, sliced diagonally into 2cm lengths
500g fresh egg noodles
½ cup hot water
2 tablespoons dark soy sauce
½ teaspoon each salt and sugar
3–4 tablespoons chopped fresh coriander

Prepare all the ingredients, then heat the oil in a wok or very large pan. Add the onion and garlic and stir-fry until the onion begins to soften. Stir in the chicken and continue to cook, stirring frequently, until the chicken is no longer pink. Add the curry powder and stir-fry for about a minute longer.

Add the carrot, broccoli and spring onions and stir-fry for 1–2 minutes until the broccoli is bright green. Add the noodles, teasing them apart a bit with your fingers as you go. Pour in the water and soy sauce, then sprinkle in the salt and sugar. Toss everything together until well combined, then cook for about 2 minutes (covering the wok/pan if you have a lid big enough) before tossing again and cooking for a further 2 minutes. By this time, the liquid should be absorbed and the noodles soft and warmed through. Add an extra ¼ cup water and cook for 2 minutes longer if the noodles are not tender.

Divide into serving bowls or plates, sprinkle with the chopped coriander and serve immediately.

Easy fish curry

I was aiming for a Malaysian-type curry with this dish. I can't actually vouch for the authenticity of the result, but it's certainly delicious and – better still – easy!

Try this served with a chunky tomato and cucumber salad, and Malaysian-style roti, which (much to my delight) are now appearing in supermarkets' refrigerated or frozen foods departments.

For 2–3 servings:
2 tablespoons canola oil
2 medium onions, finely chopped
2–3 cloves garlic, crushed, peeled and chopped
1–2 tablespoons finely chopped or grated ginger
2 teaspoons curry powder
1 tablespoon tomato paste
½ – ¾ cup water
¾ cup coconut cream
½–1 teaspoon salt
500g firm-fleshed fish fillets (snapper, monkfish, warehou etc.)
3–4 tablespoons chopped fresh coriander

Heat the oil in a large, lidded and preferably non-stick pan, then add the onions and garlic and cook over a medium-high heat, stirring occasionally, until the onions begin to brown. Stir in the chopped or grated ginger and cook for 1–2 minutes longer.

Add the curry powder and cook, stirring continuously, for another minute. Add the tomato paste, ½ cup water, the coconut cream and salt to taste. Stir until well mixed. Allow the sauce to come to the boil while you cut the fish into 2–3 cm cubes.

Gently stir the fish into the sauce, then cover the pan and cook for 2–3 minutes, or until the fish is just cooked through, adding the extra ¼ cup of water if the mixture looks too dry.

Stir in the coriander, reserving a little to garnish, then serve over steamed rice, accompanied with roti or naan and a simple salad.

Nasi goreng

In Indonesia, nasi goreng is often served as a breakfast dish, but I think this version is easily substantial enough to be served as an evening meal.

Like most fried rice dishes, nasi goreng works best if you use rice that has been cooked, allowed to cool, then fluffed up. You can either cook the rice the night before you intend to use it, storing it in the fridge until required, or pop it in the microwave before heading off to work in the morning.

One big advantage of using pre-cooked rice is that it means you can actually whip up a meal in minutes.

For 2-3 servings:
1 large onion, peeled and quartered
2 cloves garlic, crushed and peeled
1–2cm piece ginger, peeled
½ teaspoon belachan* (optional)
1 teaspoon minced red chilli (or chilli paste) (optional)
4–6 spring onions, sliced, white and green parts
    separated
2 tablespoons canola oil
2 large eggs, lightly beaten
250g pork loin steaks, cut into 1cm cubes
1 medium carrot, finely diced
2 tablespoons canola oil
3 cups cold cooked rice
200–250g cooked shrimp
2 tablespoons light soy sauce
1 teaspoon sugar
¼ – ½ cucumber, sliced, to garnish

Place the onion, garlic, and ginger plus belachan and chilli (if using) in a blender or food processor and process until they form a smooth paste.

Cut the white parts of the spring onions into slices 2–3mm thick while the first measure of oil heats in a wok or large frypan. Add the sliced spring onions and cook, stirring occasionally, until golden brown (do not overcook as they will turn bitter). Remove from the pan with a slotted spoon or fish slice and drain on paper towels. Tip the oil into a heatproof container and reserve.

Return the pan or wok to the heat, and add the lightly beaten eggs and cook to form a thin omelette. Carefully fold up the omelette and remove from the pan, then cut into 1cm slices. Return the spring onion oil to the pan and add the onion paste. Stir-fry for 2–3 minutes, add the cubed pork and stir-fry for another 3–4 minutes, then add the carrot and cook for about a minute longer.

Add the second measure of oil to the pork mixture, then stir in the rice, shrimp and spring onion greens. Toss everything together, then stir-fry until the rice and shrimp are heated through. Sprinkle in the soy sauce and sugar and toss well.

Transfer to a serving dish and arrange the sliced cucumber around the edge, then top the rice with the sliced omelette and the fried spring onions.

*Dried shrimp paste, available in stores specialising in Asian foods.

Malay beef curry

This curry does require long slow cooking, but the actual 'hands on' time is quite low and the results are definitely worth the wait!

Similarly, don't be put off by the long-looking list of ingredients – it is mainly made up of spices, which are all added in two batches. If you find you don't actually have one or two of them on hand, just leave them out – with the exception of the five-spice it will make little difference in the end.

For 4–6 servings:
1kg gravy beef, cubed
2 tablespoons ground coriander
1 tablespoon ground cumin
2 teaspoons chilli powder
2 teaspoons five-spice powder
1 teaspoon turmeric
1 teaspoon ground cinnamon
½ teaspoon ground cloves
3 tablespoons canola oil
1 medium onion, quartered and sliced
4 cardamom pods, squashed
2.5–5cm cinnamon stick
1 whole star anise
6 cloves
2 cups water
400g can coconut cream
4 medium potatoes, cubed
1–1½ cups fresh or frozen green beans (optional)
2–3 tablespoons lemon juice
1–2 teaspoons salt

Trim any obvious fat from the meat, then place the cubes in a medium bowl. Measure in the first seven spices and toss everything together so the meat is evenly coated with the spice mixture.

Heat the oil in a large heavy pot or casserole dish. Add the onion, cardamom pods, cinnamon stick, star anise and cloves and cook until the onion is soft and golden brown.

Add the spice-coated meat and cook, stirring frequently, for about 10 minutes. Stir in the water and bring to the boil, then reduce the heat to a gentle simmer, cover the pot with a close-fitting lid, and cook, stirring occasionally, for an hour.

Add the coconut cream and stir in the potatoes. Cover again and cook for a further 45–60 minutes, or until the beef is very tender. Add the beans (if using), lemon juice and salt to taste. Simmer for 5 or so minutes uncovered, until the beans are tender. Serve as is, or over steamed rice, accompanied with Malaysian roti.

Spiced lamb with tomatoes and peas

In this recipe I've used a selection of Indian spices to turn minced lamb and vegetables into something quite special, in merely half an hour!

If you don't have (or can't find) minced lamb, you can make it using minced beef – it's not quite the same but still tastes great.

For 4 servings:
1 large onion, peeled and quartered
1cm piece fresh ginger, peeled
3–4 cloves garlic, peeled
2–3 tablespoons canola oil
1 teaspoon each cumin seeds and coriander seeds, crushed
½ teaspoon each chilli powder and turmeric
500g minced lamb
400g can whole tomatoes in juice
½ cup plain unsweetened yoghurt
1 teaspoon salt
1 tablespoon garam masala
2 tablespoons lemon juice
1 fresh green chilli, thinly sliced (optional)
¼ cup chopped fresh coriander
2 cups peas, fresh or frozen

Put the roughly chopped onion, ginger, and garlic into a food processor and chop finely (or chop very finely by hand).

Heat the oil in a large non-stick pan over medium-high heat. Add the finely chopped onion mixture and stir-fry until the mixture begins to brown. Stir in the crushed cumin and coriander seeds, then the chilli powder and turmeric. Stir-fry for 1minute longer, stirring frequently.

Add the minced lamb to the pan and cook over high heat, stirring occasionally to break up any lumps, until the meat has lost its pink colour, then add the tomatoes in juice and the yoghurt. Break up the tomatoes with a fish slice or spoon.

Bring to the boil, cover and cook for 10–15 minutes, until the mixture thickens.

Stir in the salt, garam masala, lemon juice, green chilli (if using), coriander leaves and peas. Bring back to the boil, then cover again and cook for a further 5 minutes.

Serve on basmati rice, alone, or with naan bread and a selection of chutneys and pickles.

Malay beef curry

Butter chicken

Butter chicken must be one of the most popular dishes in Indian restaurants – and not without good reason.

My version is quick and simple to prepare, and actually contains no butter – my wife, Sam, actually thinks I should call this no-butter chicken!

For 2–3 servings:

2 tablespoons canola oil
1 medium onion, finely diced
2 cloves garlic, crushed, peeled and chopped
2 teaspoons curry powder (mild or hot)
1 teaspoon each ground cumin, coriander and ginger
250–300g boneless skinless chicken breasts
    or thighs, cubed
425g can tomatoes and onion
1 tablespoon tomato paste
1–2 teaspoons garam masala
¾ cup plain unsweetened yoghurt
¼ – ½ cup cream
1–2 tablespoons chopped coriander
½ –1 teaspoon salt

Heat the oil in a large pan, then add the finely diced onion and chopped garlic. Cook, stirring frequently, until the onion is soft and clear but has not browned (about 5 minutes). Add the curry powder, cumin, coriander and ginger, and cook, stirring constantly, for about a minute longer.

Add the chicken to the pan and cook, stirring occasionally, until it has lost its pinkness, then stir in the canned tomato mixture and tomato paste. Allow the mixture to boil, then reduce the heat to a gentle simmer and cook for 8–10 minutes, or until the chicken is cooked through.

Stir in the remaining ingredients, add salt to taste, and reheat without boiling. Serve over steamed rice, accompanied with poppadums and/or naan bread (naan is now available frozen in many supermarkets).

Variation:

For an extra-smooth sauce, replace the can of tomatoes and onion and tomato paste with a 300g can of condensed tomato soup plus ½ cup water and cook as above. (Tomato soup may sound like an odd addition, but it does work well!)

Tip:

Poppadums 'puff' nicely in the microwave – arrange 3 or 4 in a single layer over the paper towel covered carousel, then microwave on high for 1–2 minutes, turning once.

Curried red lentil dahl

I know that dahl dishes are often fairly plain and sometimes a little dull, but this one is definitely an exception! For such a simple recipe, it's hard to know exactly why it works so well, but it does – even those who would normally turn their noses up at the thought of red lentils will come back for more!

For 3–4 servings:

1 tablespoon canola oil
1 large onion, diced
1–2 cloves garlic, crushed, peeled and chopped
1 large bay leaf
1 teaspoon minced red chilli
2 teaspoons each curry powder and turmeric
2 teaspoons each mustard and cumin seeds
1 cup split red lentils
2 cups water
2 teaspoons instant chicken vegetable stock (optional)
2 tablespoons chopped fresh coriander
½ –1 teaspoon salt to taste

Heat the oil in a large pan, add the onion and garlic and cook, stirring frequently, until the onion has softened and is turning clear. Add the bay leaf, minced chilli, curry powder and other spices and stir-fry for 1–2 minutes.

Stir in the lentils, water and instant stock (if using). Bring the mixture to the boil, then reduce the heat to a gentle simmer and cook until the lentils are tender, about 20–25 minutes.

Remove the bay leaf, then add the salt and coriander and stir. Serve accompanied with one or more of the following: steamed basmati rice, naan bread, poppadums and your favourite chutneys, relishes or pickles.

Pad Thai (Thai-style fried noodles)

These tasty stir-fried noodles can be prepared in about 15 minutes from start to finish – it almost seems that something this good should take longer to prepare.

As with most stir-fries, things happen very fast once you actually start cooking, so it pays to prepare and measure all the ingredients before you start.

For 2–3 servings:

150–200g rice noodles
1 tablespoon canola oil
1 large egg, lightly beaten
3 cloves garlic, crushed, peeled and chopped
2 (about 200g total) boneless skinless chicken breasts, thinly sliced
1 teaspoon minced red chilli/chilli paste
200g cooked shrimp, thawed and drained if frozen
1 tablespoon canola oil
4 spring onions, sliced diagonally
3 tablespoons fish sauce
2 tablespoons rice (or wine) vinegar
1 tablespoon lime (or lemon) juice
2 tablespoons sugar
1–2 cups bean sprouts
chopped fresh coriander and roasted peanuts
    to garnish

Place the rice noodles in a large bowl, cover with boiling water and soak for 5–10 minutes or until soft and flexible, then drain well. (Check after 5 minutes as different brands seem to soften at different speeds and some get too soft if soaked for too long.)

Heat about 1 teaspoon of the oil in a large wok or frypan, then add the beaten egg and cook to form a thin omelette. As soon as the upper surface looks dry, roll or fold the omelette and remove it from the pan. Cut into 1cm ribbons and set aside.

Add the rest of the first measure of oil to the pan, then add the garlic, cook over a high heat until it begins to brown, then add the chicken and stir-fry for 3–4 minutes until chicken has lost its pink colour and is beginning to brown.

Stir in the chilli and shrimp and stir-fry for a minute longer, then add the noodles, second measure of oil and the spring onion greens. Toss to combine, then add the fish sauce, vinegar, lime (or lemon) juice and sugar.

Stir-fry until the liquid has almost disappeared, then add the bean sprouts and cook for 1 minute longer.

Serve immediately garnished with chopped coriander and peanuts.

Thai-style squid with vegetables

This spicy, Thai-inspired dish is really very simple. I like this sauce with squid for something a bit different, but it is equally good with chicken or even, omitting the marinade, vegetables alone (it's really worth trying with asparagus).

For 2–3 servings:

2 squid tubes (about 180g)
1 tablespoon each sesame oil and Kikkoman soy sauce
1cm fresh ginger, grated
2 cloves garlic
1 tablespoon each Thai fish sauce, oyster sauce and
    dark soy sauce
1 teaspoon sugar
2 tablespoons chopped fresh coriander
2 tablespoons oil
1 medium onion, quartered and sliced
½ –1 teaspoon Thai red curry paste
1 dried red chilli, deseeded and sliced (optional)
2 cups broccoli florets (or 5cm lengths of asparagus)
1 green capsicum, deseeded, quartered and sliced
1 cup button mushrooms, halved
coriander or spring onion to garnish

Halve the squid tubes lengthwise, trim and discard any remaining cartilage. Lay each half flat on a board with the inside facing upwards, and with a sharp knife score the surface into a 1cm diamond pattern. Cut into rectangles about 2 x 4cm. Place in a bowl and toss with the sesame oil, Kikkoman soy sauce, ginger and garlic.

Leave to stand while you prepare the vegetables and organise the remaining ingredients.

Measure the fish, oyster and soy sauces, sugar and coriander into a small bowl. Heat the oil in a large wok or frypan. Add the onion, curry paste and chilli (if using), stir-fry for about 1 minute, then add the broccoli (or asparagus), capsicum and mushrooms. Cook, stirring occasionally, until the broccoli is barely tender.

Add the squid and cook for 2–3 minutes, stirring frequently, then add the sauce mixture, toss, and remove from the heat. It is important not to overcook the squid or it will become chewy and tough.

Serve immediately over fragrant Thai (jasmine) rice, garnished with some additional chopped coriander or spring onions.

Pad Thai (Thai-style fried noodles)

Thai green chicken curry

For something so easy to make, a Thai green curry really does taste delicious.

Thai curry pastes are now available from most supermarkets, but the kaffir lime leaves which have a fragrance and flavour that is hard to describe may require a trip to a store specialising in Asian foods. Fresh or frozen lime leaves have the best flavour, but (soaked) dried lime leaves will do if they are all you can find.

For 3–4 servings:
2 tablespoons canola oil
1–2 tablespoons Thai green curry paste
3–4 kaffir lime leaves, cut into strips about 1cm wide
1 medium potato, cut into 1cm cubes
1 cup coconut cream
300–400g boneless skinless chicken thighs
　　or breasts, cubed
1 medium onion, sliced
2–3 zucchini, sliced
½ cup peas or green beans, fresh or frozen
150–200g can bamboo shoots, drained (optional)
¼ – ½ cup water (if required)
2 tablespoons fish sauce
1 teaspoon sugar
salt to taste
handful fresh basil leaves (optional)

Heat the oil in a frypan or wok. Stir in the curry paste and cook for 1–2 minutes, then add the lime leaves and potato and stir-fry for 1–2 minutes longer.

Carefully pour in the coconut cream, chicken and onion. Simmer for 5 minutes, stirring occasionally.

Add the vegetables and bamboo shoots (if using) and thin sauce with ¼ – ½ cup water if required. Simmer until chicken is cooked through and vegetables are just tender – about 10 minutes, then add the fish sauce and sugar. Taste and add salt if required, then stir in the basil leaves (if using).

Serve over fragrant Thai (jasmine) rice, garnished with a few extra basil leaves.

Thai-style red curry

This recipe has evolved considerably over the years I have been making it. Originally I used to use whole roasted peanuts, which I ground to a paste myself, but now it seems simpler to use peanut butter instead.

I also only ever used to use chicken mince. However, as this is not always readily available, I decided to experiment and try one using minced beef, and was very pleased with the results – I think it's equally good made this way.

For 4 servings:
2 tablespoons canola oil
1 medium onion, quartered and sliced
2 cloves garlic, crushed, peeled and chopped
2–3 tablespoons Thai red curry paste*
2–3 kaffir lime leaves (soaked, if dried), chopped
　　(optional)
500g minced chicken or lean beef
400g can coconut cream (or 1 cup coconut cream plus
　　1 cup chicken or beef stock)
¼ cup crunchy peanut butter
½ cup water (if required)
2 tablespoons fish sauce
½ –1 teaspoon each salt and sugar
2–3 tablespoons chopped coriander
1–2 cups sliced or diced vegetables (e.g. zucchini,
　　cauliflower or broccoli florets, carrots, beans, peas)
coriander, spring onions and/or roasted peanuts
　　to garnish

Heat the oil in a large pan, add the onion and garlic and cook, stirring frequently until the onion is soft. Stir in the red curry paste and lime leaves (if using) and cook for about 1 minute longer, then add the minced chicken or beef. Continue to cook, stirring frequently and breaking up any lumps until the mince has lost its pink colour.

Add the coconut cream (or coconut cream-stock mixture) and stir in the peanut butter. Reduce the heat to a gentle simmer and cook for 6–8 minutes, stirring occasionally. If the mixture looks too dry during this time, add the extra water.

Add the remaining seasonings and the prepared vegetables. Stir to combine then cook until the vegetables are just tender.

Serve on rice garnished with a little extra chopped coriander (or spring onions) and/or some chopped roasted peanuts.

*The strength and 'hotness' of red curry paste varies from brand to brand. If you are new to Thai cooking, or are using a different paste to usual it is prudent to err on the side of caution!

Thai green chicken curry

Pork with beans and beer

This is a tasty variant on the chilli con carne theme – I make it with pork for something a little different, but if you like you can revert to the more 'traditional' beef. Being a casserole it does take a while to cook, but it actually only needs 15–20 minutes of hands-on time.

Chipotles chillies have a wonderful smoky flavour – they are sometimes sold canned in sauce or dried and ground to a powder. If you ever see chipotle powder, it is worth buying to have a play with, it's great added to salsa etc. Don't worry if you can't find it, you can use chilli powder instead, although obviously you won't get the smoky flavour.

For 4–6 servings:

2 tablespoons olive (or canola) oil
750g lean pork, cubed (I use leg steaks, cubed)
2 medium onions, quartered and sliced
4 cloves garlic, crushed, peeled and chopped
1 large green capsicum, deseeded and diced
2–3 sticks celery, thinly sliced (optional)
2 teaspoons chipotle (or chilli) powder
2 teaspoons ground cumin
1 teaspoon oregano
440g can red kidney beans, drained and rinsed
2 x 400g cans whole tomatoes in juice
355ml can or bottle (about 1½ cups) beer
about 1 teaspoon salt
chopped coriander or parsley to garnish (optional)

Heat the oil in a large heavy casserole dish. Add the pork and cook over a high heat, stirring occasionally, for 5–10 minutes until lightly browned. Stir in the onions, garlic, capsicum and celery (if using) and cook, stirring frequently, until the onions are soft, about 5 minutes.

Add the chipotle or chilli powder, cumin and oregano and cook for about a minute longer, then add the kidney beans, tomatoes and their juice and the beer. Break up the whole tomatoes and stir to combine.

Bring the casserole to the boil then reduce the heat to low and simmer uncovered, stirring occasionally, for about 1½ hours or until the meat is very tender. Season to taste with salt.

Serve spooned into deep bowls, garnished with chopped herbs if desired, and accompanied with chunks of crusty bread, or ladle over steamed rice.

Pork with beans and beer

Chicken and vegetable casserole

I'm sure that in my grandmother's day this sort of casserole would have been made with an older 'boiling fowl' that required long, slow cooking to make it palatable, but with today's tender poultry it can actually be cooked in a surprisingly short time.

For 4 servings:
2 tablespoons olive (or canola) oil
1.2–1.5kg chicken pieces
2 onions, quartered and sliced
3 cloves garlic, crushed, peeled and chopped
2–3 sticks celery, cut into 1cm slices
3 medium carrots, cut into 1cm slices
2 bay leaves
1 teaspoon thyme
½ teaspoon tarragon
2½ cups water
2 teaspoons instant chicken stock
750g small-medium potatoes, scrubbed
2 tablespoons cornflour mixed with 2 tablespoons water
½–1 teaspoon salt
pepper to taste
2–3 tablespoons chopped fresh parsley

Turn the oven on to 180°C. Heat the oil over a high heat in a large casserole dish, then working in batches that will fit comfortably in the pot, brown the chicken pieces on all sides, remove and set aside. Reduce the heat a little and add the onions and garlic to the pan and cook, stirring frequently to prevent browning, until the onions have softened, then add the celery and carrots and cook for a few minutes longer.

Return the chicken to the pot, and add the herbs, water, and instant chicken stock. Cut larger potatoes into quarters or eighths, halve (or leave whole) smaller potatoes and add these to the pot. Stir gently to mix, then bring to the boil.

Cover the casserole and transfer to the oven. Cook at 180°C for about 40 minutes, stirring once or twice, until the chicken is very tender and the potatoes are cooked through.

Return the casserole to the stove. Remove and set aside the chicken pieces, then add the cornflour and water mixed to a thin paste to the casserole. Stir gently to combine, then heat until the sauce thickens. Return the chicken pieces to the sauce then season to taste with salt and pepper and add the chopped parsley.

Keep warm until required, or serve immediately. A crusty bread roll (or two) to mop up the gravy makes an ideal accompaniment.

Moussaka

This is a simplified version of the Greek dish. It retains the traditional layers of eggplant and minced meat but I have grilled rather than fried the eggplant, and used a yoghurt rather than roux-based topping. Both of these changes simplify the overall process and I'm sure you'll agree the result is delicious.

For 4–6 servings:
500g (2 medium) eggplant
3–4 tablespoons olive oil
1 tablespoon olive oil
1 medium onion, diced
2 cloves garlic, crushed, peeled and chopped
500g minced lamb or beef
2 tablespoons tomato paste
½ cup red wine or stock
1 tablespoon chopped fresh oregano (or 1 teaspoon dried oregano)
2–3 tablespoons chopped fresh parsley
¼ teaspoon each ground allspice and cinnamon
1 teaspoon salt
freshly ground pepper to taste
2 tablespoons dried breadcrumbs
2 cups plain unsweetened yoghurt
2 large eggs
1 cup grated tasty cheese

Cut the unpeeled eggplant/s lengthwise into 12mm thick slices. Brush both sides lightly with oil and arrange the slices on a baking tray. Grill them about 10cm from the heat, turning once, until browned on both sides (about 5 minutes per side).

While the eggplant cooks, heat the second measure of oil in a large pan, then add the onion and garlic, along with the mince. Cook, stirring frequently, until the mince is crumbly and is beginning to brown. Stir in the tomato paste, red wine (or stock) and seasonings. Simmer the mixture over a low heat for 8–10 minutes.

Lightly oil a 20 x 30cm casserole dish then sprinkle the bottom with the breadcrumbs. Arrange half of the browned eggplant in an even layer over the bottom of the dish, spread the mince mixture evenly over this, then layer the remaining eggplant over the top.

Whisk together the yoghurt and eggs, pour this mixture over the top of the layered eggplant and mince, then sprinkle with the grated cheese. Bake at 200°C for 15–20 minutes, or until the topping is set and has turned golden brown.

Serve with a green or tomato salad and crusty bread with a little olive oil for dipping.

Moroccan chicken with spicy rice pilaf

Technically this would have to be termed a 'two-dish' meal, as although the chicken and rice are baked at the same time, they are cooked in separate dishes.

For 4 servings:
1 large onion, quartered
3–4 cloves garlic
3 tablespoons olive oil
1 tablespoon tomato paste
1 teaspoon each ground cumin and paprika
½ teaspoon each ground ginger and salt
2 tablespoons chopped coriander
2 lemons, cut lengthwise into 8 wedges
4 large bone-in chicken pieces or 8 drumsticks
(about 1kg total)
15–20 black olives
chopped fresh coriander to garnish

Place the onion and garlic in a food processor or blender and chop finely. Add the next seven ingredients and the juice of 1 of the lemons and mix into a thick paste.

Arrange the chicken in a large shallow casserole dish and spread the paste mixture evenly on all sides of the chicken. Place the lemon wedges between pieces of chicken with the olives.

Cover and leave to stand for 1–2 hours if possible (or refrigerate overnight). When ready to cook, heat oven to 180°C (or 170°C if using fan-bake). Cover loosely with foil and bake for 30 minutes, then cook uncovered for another 30 minutes.

Serve, garnished with coriander, on a bed of Spicy Rice Pilaf (below), or plain rice or couscous and a green salad.

Variation:

For authenticity, replace the lemon wedges with the skin of one preserved, salted lemon, if you can find any.

Spicy Rice Pilaf

For 4 servings:
2 tablespoons olive oil
1 medium onion, diced
2 cloves garlic, crushed, peeled and chopped
¼ cup slivered almonds or pine nuts
¼ cup currants
½ teaspoon each cumin, coriander, cinnamon
and chilli powder
1 cup long-grain rice
1 medium carrot, finely diced
grated rind of 1 lemon (optional)
3 cups boiling water plus 3 teaspoons instant
chicken stock

Heat the oil in a flame-proof casserole dish, add the onion and garlic and cook until the onion is soft. Stir in the nuts and currants and cook, stirring frequently, until the nuts are golden brown.

Add the spices, rice and carrot and cook for about a minute longer then add the lemon rind (if using), the boiling water and instant stock.

Bring to the boil, then cover with a close fitting lid and place in the oven with the chicken and cook, stirring once or twice, for 45–60 minutes until the rice is cooked through and the liquid absorbed.

Tuscan-style pork with beans

It might just be me, but I think that there is something very comfort food-ish about succulent pork chops simmered in this well flavoured tomato and bean mixture.

For 2 servings:

2 tablespoons flour
½ teaspoon each ground black pepper and paprika
¼ teaspoon each garlic salt and celery salt
2 tablespoons olive oil
2 large (400–500g total) pork loin chops
1 medium onion, diced
2–3 cloves garlic, crushed, peeled and chopped
1 large red capsicum, deseeded and diced
3 medium tomatoes, diced
2 tablespoons chopped fresh herbs (sage and thyme)*
300g can butter beans, drained and rinsed
½ cup chicken stock (or ½ cup water plus 1 teaspoon
    instant chicken stock)
salt and pepper to taste
extra herbs to garnish

Mix the first five ingredients together in a shallow dish or bowl. Heat the oil in a large lidded pan over a high heat. Coat both sides of the pork chops with the seasoned flour, then place the chops in the heated pan and cook for 2 minutes each side or until golden brown. Lift the chops from the pan and set aside.

Add the onion and garlic to the pan and cook, stirring frequently, until the onion is soft. Stir in the capsicum and continue to cook until the onion begins to brown. Mix in the diced tomatoes and herbs and simmer for 2–3 minutes or until the tomatoes begin to break down, then add the beans and stock (or water plus instant stock). Stir gently to combine, then nestle the chops into the bean mixture.

Reduce the heat to a gentle simmer, cover the pan and cook for 15–20 minutes, turning the chops once. Check occasionally to see that the mixture hasn't dried out, adding a little more water if required.

Season to taste with salt and pepper, then spoon the bean mixture onto plates and top with the chops. Garnish with a sprig of thyme or sage leaves, and serve with a chunk of bread to mop up any juices.

*Dried sage seems to have a quite different flavour to fresh sage, but if you can only find dried herbs use ½ teaspoon sage and 1 teaspoon thyme.

Spicy beef ragout with vegetables

This is a fairly traditional beef stew, livened up with the addition of some whole spices. Although it does require long slow cooking, it is quick to prepare, and is equally good served with rice, pasta or potatoes.

For 3–4 servings:

400–500g lean chuck steak, cubed
2 tablespoons flour
2 tablespoons olive oil
3 bay leaves
4–5 whole allspice
4–5 whole cloves
½ teaspoon black peppercorns
1 star anise
1 medium onion, cut into eighths
2 medium carrots, thickly sliced
100g button mushrooms
1 red capsicum, deseeded and coarsely chopped
400g can whole tomatoes in juice
½ cup red wine
salt and pepper to taste

Sprinkle the cubed steak with the flour, then toss so the pieces are evenly coated.

Heat the oil in a large (lidded) casserole dish or heavy pot. Add the cubed beef and cook, stirring occasionally, until the pieces are lightly browned on all sides. Add the bay leaves, spices, and fresh vegetables. Cook, stirring frequently, for another 3–4 minutes.

Add the tomatoes in their juice and the red wine. Allow the mixture to come to the boil, then reduce the heat to a very gentle simmer and cook, stirring occasionally, for 1½–2 hours, or until the beef is very tender. Add a little extra liquid (water or wine) if the sauce looks too dry. Season to taste with salt and pepper.

When the meat is cooked remove the bay leaves and any obvious whole spices. Serve with rice, pasta or potatoes and garnish with a little chopped parsley.

Beef and mushroom casserole

This recipe makes a delicious large casserole. It is great for entertaining and makes enough for several smaller family meals – simply freeze the extra in conveniently sized portions for those evenings when you just can't be bothered cooking.

Gravy beef does take longer to cook than some other cuts, but it really does give a deep, rich flavour.

For 6–8 servings:
4 dried Chinese mushrooms,* sliced
¼ cup boiling water
1.5kg gravy beef, cubed
2 tablespoons olive (or canola) oil
3 medium onions, quartered and sliced
1 tablespoon olive (or canola) oil
1 tablespoon sugar
¼ cup balsamic vinegar
2 x 400g cans whole tomatoes in juice
½ cup red wine (or water)
250–400g button mushrooms, halved
salt and pepper to taste

Place the dried mushrooms in a small bowl or cup and cover with the boiling water, then set aside to soak.

Trim any visible fat from the meat, then heat the first measure of oil in a large heavy casserole dish. Working in 3 or 4 batches, add the meat to the casserole dish and brown the cubes on all sides, then remove and set aside. Repeat until all the meat has been browned.

Add the remaining measure of oil to the casserole dish, then add the onions and cook, stirring occasionally, until the onions have softened. Add the sugar and balsamic vinegar and continue to cook until the onions are a rich brown colour.

Add the tomatoes in their juice and red wine (or water), then stir, breaking up the whole tomatoes. Add the browned beef, soaked mushrooms (plus liquid) and the button mushrooms to the casserole and stir to mix. Allow the mixture to come to the boil then reduce the heat to very low. Cover the casserole dish with a close-fitting lid and cook for 1½–2 hours, stirring every now and then, until the beef is very tender.

Serve with boiled or mashed potatoes, pasta (my favourite) or rice, and the steamed vegetable/s of your choice.

*Available from shops specialising in Asian foods or bulk-bins of some supermarkets.

Bread-topped bean casserole

There is something very warming about the way the rich dark filling of this casserole hides under a crisp golden crust – it also makes the whole thing look far more elegant and complex than it really is!

For 4 large servings:
2 tablespoons olive or canola oil
1 large onion, peeled, quartered and sliced
2 cloves garlic, crushed, peeled and chopped
1 medium carrot, quartered and sliced
1 teaspoon sugar
½ each red and green capsicum, deseeded and sliced
6 (about 150g) mushrooms, quartered
1 tablespoon flour
½ cup water
1 tablespoon tomato paste
½ teaspoon basil
¼ teaspoon thyme
440g can red kidney beans, drained and rinsed
½ –1 teaspoon salt
black pepper to taste
½ loaf French bread
1–2 tablespoons olive oil
½ –1 cup grated cheese

Heat the oil in a large pan, then add the onions, garlic and carrot and cook, stirring frequently, until the onions are soft and clear. Add the sugar, capsicums and mushrooms and continue to cook, stirring frequently, until the onions have browned. Stir in the flour and cook for a minute longer, then add the water, tomato paste and herbs. Mix in the beans and season to taste with salt and pepper.

Simmer gently for about 5 minutes then transfer to a lightly oiled or non-stick sprayed 20 x 25cm casserole dish. The filling can be prepared ahead to this stage.

Turn the oven on to preheat to 225°C, then cut the bread into 1–1.5cm thick slices, and pour the second measure of oil into a small shallow dish or saucer. Lightly dip one side of each bread slice into the oil (it should just be moistened with oil, not soaked) and arrange the slices oiled side up, in an overlapping pattern, over the top of the filling mixture until it is all covered.

Sprinkle the bread topping with the grated cheese using more or less to taste, then bake at 225°C for 10–15 minutes until the filling is hot and the crust golden brown. Serve with boiled or mashed potatoes, some lightly cooked winter vegetables or even a salad.

Chicken and vegetable couscous

This recipe will fill your kitchen with wonderful fragrant aromas as it cooks!

In traditional versions, the couscous is steamed over the chicken mixture as it cooks, hence the name. If, however, you are using quick-cooking couscous (now the most common sort), you only need to soak it briefly in boiling water.

For 4–6 servings:

2 tablespoons olive oil
2 medium onions, quartered and sliced
2–3 cloves garlic, crushed, peeled and chopped
300–400g boneless skinless chicken breast, sliced
1 teaspoon each ground coriander, cumin and turmeric
½ teaspoon each salt and chilli powder
¼ teaspoon each ground cloves and allspice
400g can whole tomatoes in juice
300g can chickpeas, drained and rinsed
2–3 medium potatoes, cubed
2 carrots, cubed
2 cups vegetables (diced kumara, zucchini, peas etc.)
1 cup quick-cooking couscous
1–1½ cups boiling water
1 teaspoon instant chicken stock

Heat the oil in a large, lidded frypan, then add the onions and garlic and cook until the onions are soft and transparent. Add the chicken and stir-fry until no longer pink, then add the next seven ingredients and cook for about a minute longer, stirring continuously.

Chop the tomatoes and add with their juice. Stir in the chickpeas, potatoes and carrots. Cover the pot or pan and simmer for 15–20 minutes, adding the remaining vegetables at intervals (the slower cooking ones first), so that all are cooked at the same time.

While the chicken and vegetable mixture simmers, measure the couscous into a large shallow bowl and add the boiling water and stock powder. (I like my couscous fairly dry so I use the smaller quantity of water, but some people like it a bit moister, so add the extra if you like.) Stir, then cover and leave to stand.

When the chicken and vegetables are cooked, fluff the couscous with a fork then spread it over a large plate or platter and top with the cooked chicken and vegetable mixture. Serve alone or accompany with bread and a salad.

Spicy Indian mince and rice

This Indian flavoured mince and rice dish is a delicious one-pan meal. Like many Indian-style recipes the ingredients list may look long, but this is due to the spices used which are mainly added at the same time, so it really is quite simple to prepare.

For 4 servings:

2–3 tablespoons canola oil
1 large onion
2 cloves garlic
2 teaspoons each curry powder and ground ginger
½ teaspoon each chilli powder, ground cinnamon and whole cloves
1 teaspoon black peppercorns
2 bay leaves
3–4 cardamom pods, crushed (optional)
400–500g lamb or beef mince
1 cup long-grain or basmati rice
400g can whole tomatoes in juice
2 cups hot water
2 teaspoons instant chicken or beef stock
2 teaspoons garam masala
1 teaspoon salt
¼ cup each toasted whole or slivered almonds and currants (optional)
1–2 tablespoons chopped coriander

Heat the oil in a very large pan (an electric frypan is ideal). Add the chopped onion and garlic and cook, stirring frequently, for about 5 minutes, or until the onion begins to brown. Add the next seven ingredients (and the cardamom pods if using) and cook for 1–2 minutes longer, then stir in the mince.

Continue to cook, stirring frequently to break up any lumps, until the mince has lost its pink colour, then add the rice, the tomatoes in their juice, the water and stock. Break up the tomatoes and bring the mixture to the boil, then reduce the heat to a gentle simmer.

Cover and cook, stirring occasionally, for about 15 minutes, or until the rice is tender. Add the garam masala and salt to taste.

If using them, brown the almonds and 'puff up' the currants by heating them in a little oil in a small pot or frypan, then stir them into the mixture with the chopped coriander leaves.

Cook for 1–2 minutes longer before serving as is, or accompanied by poppadums or other Indian breads.

Coq au vin

This is my version of one of the classic French casseroles. It is surprisingly simple to prepare and can be served dressed up or down to suit your needs.

For 4–6 servings:
3–4 tablespoons flour
salt and pepper
1.2–1.5kg chicken pieces
2 tablespoons olive oil
2–3 tablespoons (25g) butter
12–15 (400–500g) pickling onions, peeled
2–3 cloves garlic, crushed, peeled and chopped
250–300g small button mushrooms
2–3 bay leaves
1 teaspoon thyme
1½ cups red wine
1 tablespoon sugar
2 teaspoons cornflour
1–2 tablespoons cold water
2–3 tablespoons chopped fresh parsley
salt and pepper to taste

Preheat the oven to 180°C. Measure the flour into a large plastic bag and season with salt and pepper. Add half of the chicken pieces and toss well to coat, then remove from bag and repeat process with the remaining chicken pieces.

Heat the oil and butter over a high heat in a large heavy casserole dish. Working in batches that will fit comfortably into the casserole, fry the chicken pieces until golden brown on all sides. Remove browned chicken and set aside.

Reduce heat and add the onions to the casserole and cook, stirring occasionally, until the onions have softened, about 5 minutes. Add garlic and cook for 1 minute longer, then add the mushrooms and continue to cook until these have softened.

Return the chicken to the casserole, then add the bay leaves, thyme, red wine and sugar. Stir gently to combine, then bring to the boil. Cover with a close-fitting lid, then place in the oven and cook for about 40–60 minutes, or until the chicken is very tender.

Remove the chicken pieces and return the casserole dish to the stovetop. Mix the cornflour to a paste with the water then stir this into the casserole. Heat until the liquid thickens, then add the chopped parsley (reserving a little to garnish) and season to taste with salt and pepper.

Return the chicken to the casserole dish and mix gently. Keep hot until required. (Alternatively, if serving immediately, divide chicken pieces between warmed serving plates and spoon the vegetable-sauce mixture over the top.)

Serve garnished with the remaining parsley and accompanied with chunks of crusty French bread, and/or boiled potatoes and lightly cooked seasonal vegetables.

Irish stew

This simple stew requires a lengthy cooking time, but the preparation really couldn't be much simpler, as there is no pre-cooking involved. Original Irish stews were made with mutton, but when lamb is reasonably priced, why not use it instead?

For 4–6 servings:
2–3 (about 500g) medium onions, halved and sliced
2–3 sticks celery, cut diagonally into 1cm slices
3 medium carrots, cut into 1cm slices
8 (about 1.5kg) lamb shoulder chops
4–5 medium (about 1kg total) potatoes, peeled and thinly sliced
about 1 teaspoon each salt, thyme and rosemary
black pepper
4–5 cups hot water plus 3 teaspoons instant chicken stock
2–3 tablespoons cornflour mixed with 2 tablespoons water (optional)
2–3 tablespoons chopped parsley

Preheat the oven to 180°C. Spread about half of the onions, celery and carrots over the bottom of a very large casserole dish. Arrange 4 of the chops in a single layer over the vegetables then cover these with about half of the potato slices. Sprinkle with half of the salt, thyme and rosemary and add a generous grind of pepper.

Repeat the layering process, so you finish with another layer of seasoned potatoes. Pour in enough of the stock mixture to just cover the top layer. Place the lid on the casserole, then place in the oven and cook at 180°C for 2–2½ hours.

Remove from the oven and stir gently to mix the layers. If you want to thicken the liquid, mix the cornflour to a thin paste with water and stir into the casserole, then heat gently on the stove until the liquid has thickened.

Sprinkle with the chopped parsley just before serving. Accompany with the lightly cooked green vegetable of your choice and, if you can find it, a thick wedge of Irish soda bread.

Corn chip casserole

My wife, Sam, came up with the idea for this delicious if unusual sounding recipe. Glancing at the ingredients may make you think of nachos, but cooked like this the corn chips soften and take on a quite different character.

For 4 servings:

2 tablespoons olive or canola oil
1 medium onion, peeled, quartered and sliced
2 cloves garlic, peeled and chopped
200–300g boneless skinless chicken breast, cubed or sliced
1 medium red or green capsicum, deseeded and sliced
1 teaspoon each ground cumin and oregano
½ teaspoon chilli powder
½ teaspoon salt
440g can red kidney beans, drained and rinsed
1 large avocado, peeled and diced
2–3 tablespoons chopped fresh coriander
juice ½ lemon or 1 lime
3 tablespoons (25g) butter
3 tablespoons flour
1½ cups milk
1 cup grated tasty cheese
½ teaspoon ground cumin
½ teaspoon oregano (optional)
about 150g corn chips
½ cup grated cheese
paprika to dust

Heat the oil in a large pan, add the onion and garlic and sauté for 1–2 minutes then add the chicken and capsicum. Continue to cook, stirring frequently, until the onion is soft and turning clear and the chicken has lost its pink colour. Remove the pan from the heat and stir in the seasonings, kidney beans, diced avocado, coriander and the lemon (or lime) juice. Leave to stand while you prepare the sauce.

Melt the butter in a medium pot, add the flour and stir to make a smooth paste. Cook for 1 minute, stirring continuously, then add half of the milk. Continue stirring until the mixture thickens and comes to the boil, ensuring there are no lumps. Add the remaining milk and let the sauce thicken and boil again. Remove from the heat and stir in the cheese and extra seasonings (if using).

Turn the oven on to preheat to 220°C. Arrange half of the corn chips in a layer over the bottom of a shallow (25 x 30 cm) casserole dish. Cover these with the chicken-bean mixture, then cover this with the remaining corn chips.

Pour the cheese sauce evenly over the layered mixture, then sprinkle with the additional grated cheese and dust with paprika. Bake at 220°C for 15–20 minutes or until the top is golden brown.

Serve alone, or with rice and a shredded lettuce salad.

Casseroled lamb shanks

The quantities here are only for two – if you want to make more, simply multiply the quantities accordingly.

For 2 servings:

1 tablespoon olive (or canola) oil
2 lamb shanks
1 medium onion, sliced
2 cloves garlic, crushed, peeled and chopped
250–300g button mushrooms
2 bay leaves
½ teaspoon each dried thyme and marjoram
½ cup white wine
1 cup water
1 teaspoon instant chicken stock
2–3 medium potatoes, quartered (or 10 –12 whole baby potatoes)
2 medium carrots, in 1cm slices (or 10 –12 whole baby carrots)
salt and pepper to taste

Heat the oil in a medium casserole dish or large lidded frypan. Add the lamb shanks and brown on all sides. Remove the shanks and set aside.

Add the onion and garlic to the pan and cook, stirring occasionally, until the onion has softened and is just beginning to brown. Stir in the mushrooms (leave small mushrooms whole and halve or slice larger ones), bay leaves, thyme and marjoram and continue to cook until the mushrooms wilt.

Return the shanks to the pan and add the wine, water and instant stock. Stir to combine then reduce the heat to a gentle simmer and cook for 1 hour or until the shanks are tender. Lift the shanks from the casserole, stir the potatoes and carrots into the liquid, then place the shanks on top. Cover the casserole and cook for a further 45 minutes, stirring once or twice.

Season to taste with salt and pepper then serve.

Casseroled lamb shanks

Herb-mustard crusted lamb racks with roasted vegetables

These delicious little lamb racks cook so fast that you will have to start the vegetables first.

This is not strictly a one-dish meal as you will probably need to use two roasting pans or trays as the potatoes brown best when spread out in a single layer.

For 3–4 servings:

2 x 10cm sprigs rosemary
2–3 x 10cm sprigs mint
2–3 cloves garlic, peeled
2 tablespoons wholegrain or smooth Dijon-style mustard
2 tablespoons olive oil
1 tablespoon balsamic vinegar
2–3 French cut (chined) lamb racks
800–900g potatoes
1 medium onion
2–3 medium carrots
1 bunch (250g) thin asparagus (optional)
2–3 tablespoons olive oil
2 cloves garlic, crushed, peeled and chopped
1 red capsicum, deseeded and cut into eighths

Place the first six ingredients in a blender or food processor and blend or process until more or less smooth. Put the lamb racks and mustard mixture in an unpunctured plastic bag. Massage the bag so the lamb is evenly coated with the paste, then leave to stand for at least 15 minutes (you can prepare the remaining ingredients and preheat the oven in this time).

Turn the oven on to preheat to 225°C. Cut the potatoes into 1cm slices then place them in a large pot of salted boiling water and boil gently for 6 minutes. Drain well and set aside. Halve and peel the onion, without removing the root end, then cut each half into 4–6 wedges. Peel or scrub the carrots and halve lengthwise, cut each half (lengthwise) into 4–6 thin wedges. Remove any tough ends from the asparagus (if using).

Place a roasting pan or sponge roll tin in the oven to preheat. Put the potatoes and onion in a large plastic bag, then add 2 tablespoons of olive oil and the garlic and toss gently until coated with oil. Remove the hot pan from the oven and arrange the potatoes and onion in a more or less single layer over the bottom of the pan. Return pan to oven and cook for 5 minutes.

Meanwhile add the carrots and other vegetables to the bag (adding the extra tablespoon of oil if required). Toss to coat then arrange over the bottom of the second pan. Add the lamb racks, spreading them with any excess marinade paste, then place in the oven and cook at 225°C for 15–20 minutes, depending on how rare you like the lamb.

Remove lamb and vegetables from the oven, allow the lamb to stand while you divide the vegetables between warmed plates. Slice the racks into individual cutlets, add these to the plates and serve immediately.

Herb-mustard crusted lamb racks with roasted vegetables

Roast beef with potatoes

Roasts don't really get much simpler than this! Spend about 10–15 minutes getting it ready then put it in the oven and come back in an hour.

If you can, let the beef come up to room temperature before cooking it – the French swear that this, along with resting the meat before carving, is one of the keys to tenderness.

For 4–6 servings:
1.2–1.5kg beef topside roast
2 cloves garlic, peeled and sliced
2 tablespoons Dijon mustard
1 tablespoon each olive oil and dark soy sauce
1–2 teaspoons fresh or dried thyme (optional)
1–2 teaspoons fresh or dried rosemary, chopped
   (optional)
1–1.2kg potatoes, scrubbed
1 cup boiling water plus 1 teaspoon chicken stock
2 cloves garlic, crushed, peeled and chopped
2 tablespoons olive oil
salt and pepper to taste

Pierce the beef at intervals with a sharp knife and insert a sliver of garlic into each hole. Measure the mustard, oil, soy sauce and herbs (if using) into a large plastic bag. Massage the bag to mix them, then add the beef. Massage the bag again so the paste covers the entire roast. Leave to stand for at least 15 minutes or longer if possible (up to 24 hours if refrigerated).

Preheat the oven to 180°C. Cut the potatoes into 1–1.5cm thick slices, then arrange the overlapping slices in the bottom of a small roasting pan or shallow casserole dish. Pour in the boiling stock mixture, then sprinkle them with the chopped garlic, olive oil and salt and pepper to taste.

Place the beef on a wire rack and rest it over the potatoes, then place in the oven and cook for 1–1¼ hours, depending on how well done you like the beef. (Use a meat thermometer if you have one – the temperature at the thickest part should be 50°C for rare or 60°C for medium.) Stand the cooked beef in a warm place for 10–15 minutes before carving, collecting any juices to add to the gravy.

Serve on warmed plates accompanied with gravy and one or more lightly cooked seasonal vegetables.

Note:
To make a tangy gravy heat 1–2 tablespoons of Dijon mustard (smooth or whole grain), ½ cup red wine and ½ cup water, vegetable cooking liquid or stock and any juices collected during resting or carving.

30-minute roast chicken and vegetables

I know it seems hard to believe, but it is possible to roast chicken pieces, with vegetables, so that you have a meal 'on the table' in about 30 minutes. One of the key factors is a very hot oven, so as soon as you think about starting to prepare the ingredients, turn the oven on to preheat.

I have given this recipe in quantities suited for two people, but all the quantities can be multiplied for larger numbers, depending on oven space. For fastest cooking the vegetables and chicken should be arranged in a single layer over the bottom of a roasting pan, but you can use more than one tray in most ovens.

For 2 servings:
2 tablespoons olive oil
1 tablespoon balsamic vinegar
1–2 cloves garlic, peeled and chopped
1 teaspoon each paprika and cumin
2 whole (drumstick and thigh) chicken legs
2–3 medium potatoes, each in 6–8 thin wedges
1 medium kumara, cut into 6–8 thin wedges
about 250g pumpkin, sliced about 1cm thick
1 head (bulb) garlic (optional)
1 medium onion, cut into 6–8 thin wedges
1 red capsicum, deseeded and quartered
4–6 mushrooms
2 medium zucchini, quartered lengthwise

Turn the oven on to preheat to 225°C. Measure the first five ingredients into a large plastic bag and massage to mix. Add the chicken pieces and toss to coat in the seasoning mixture, then remove and place on a lightly oiled (or teflon or baking paper lined) sponge roll tin or roasting pan.

Put the potatoes and kumara into the bag, toss to coat, then arrange these around the chicken. Place the tray in the oven and set the timer for 30 minutes.

After about 5 minutes, toss the pumpkin, garlic (if using), onion wedges and capsicum in the seasoning mixture and add them to the roasting pan. After another 5 minutes coat and add the remaining vegetables.

When the chicken has cooked for 30 minutes, pierce it at the thickest part with a sharp knife or skewer. If the juices run clear it is cooked and ready to serve, if not, cook for another 5 minutes and test again. Arrange the chicken and vegetables on warmed plates and serve.

Provencal-style roast pork with orange-baked kumara

Serving kumara with Provencal-style pork is certainly crossing food from two completely different cultures, but I think they go well together. Add the green vegetable of your choice for a really interesting meal.

For 4–6 servings:
1.2–1.5kg pork loin (or leg) roast, boned and rolled
6–8 fresh sage leaves
4 cloves garlic, crushed peeled and sliced
about 1 tablespoon fresh thyme (1–2 teaspoons dried)
1–2 bay leaves, crushed (optional)
1–2 tablespoons olive oil
¼ cup each white wine and water
2 tablespoons olive oil
salt and pepper

Pierce the pork at intervals with a sharp knife and poke half a sage leaf and a sliver of garlic into each hole. Rub the roast with the remaining garlic, thyme, bay leaves (if using) and the first measure of olive oil. Place the meat in a plastic bag and leave to stand for at least 30 minutes. (Refrigerate overnight, then stand at room temperature for 30 minutes before cooking, if possible.)

Preheat the oven to 180°C. Place the pork in an ovenproof casserole or small roasting pan and pour in the wine, water and second measure of olive oil.

Place the roast in the oven and cook for 35–40 minutes per 500g meat, adding the kumara when there is about an hour to go.

Serve the pork with the kumara and cooked green vegetables.

Orange-Baked Kumara

For 6 servings:
1kg (about 4 medium) kumara
2 cloves garlic, crushed, peeled and chopped
50g butter
grated rind of 1 orange
¼ cup brown sugar
¼ cup orange juice
¼ cup white wine
½ teaspoon salt
black pepper to taste

Peel the kumara then cut into slices about 1cm thick. Arrange the slices in a large, flat ovenware dish (not the same dish as the roast pork) which has been non-stick sprayed or lightly oiled and sprinkle with the garlic.

Place the butter in a small bowl and warm until melted. Add remaining ingredients to the bowl and heat until the sugar dissolves, then pour the mixture over the kumara. Shake the dish gently, then cover with a close fitting lid or foil and bake at 180°C for about 30 minutes then uncover and stir gently. Bake uncovered for a further 30 minutes, stirring every 10 minutes, or until the kumara are golden brown and the syrup is thick. Serve immediately.

Stuffed mushrooms

These tasty stuffed mushrooms are very versatile – larger mushrooms make a great vegetarian main, or you can use more, smaller mushrooms and serve them as a starter or finger food. Either way, the filling can be prepared ahead in minutes and the mushrooms baked when required.

For 3–4 large servings or 6–8 'starters':
2 slices wholemeal bread
1 clove garlic, peeled
1 tablespoon each olive oil, pesto and
    grated parmesan cheese
2–3 tablespoons chopped black olives
½ teaspoon chopped fresh thyme (or ¼ teaspoon dried)
¼ – ½ teaspoon salt
¼ cup pine nuts
8 large (10–12cm) flat, or 12–16 smaller (6–8cm)
    mushrooms
black pepper to taste

Tear the bread into small pieces and crumb in a food processor. Add the garlic and process briefly. Add the next six ingredients, and process until just mixed (the mixture should stay crumbly, not turn to paste). Tip in the pine nuts and process again to mix evenly.

Remove and discard the mushroom stems. Arrange the mushrooms (gills up) in a single layer over the bottom of a sponge roll tin or roasting pan. Spoon the filling into the caps, dividing it evenly between the mushrooms and leaving it sitting 'fluffed-up' rather than packed down. Sprinkle with black pepper.

Bake at 220°C for 12–15 minutes, or until the filling is golden brown. Remove from the oven and leave to stand for about 5 minutes before serving.

Serve as is for a starter, or accompany with a salad and bread as a main.

Lemon-garlic-herb roasted chicken

I don't know what makes a roast chicken dinner seem so special, but I can't think of anyone (vegetarians excepted) who isn't pleased to see one at the table. This is my favourite version for two reasons: it tastes great and it's really easy!

For 4–6 servings:

1 medium to large (1.5–1.8kg) chicken
1 large or 2 small lemons
3–4 cloves garlic, crushed and peeled
2–3 sprigs each fresh thyme and tarragon (or rosemary)
1–2 tablespoons olive oil
salt and pepper
1–1.5kg roasting vegetables (potatoes, kumara,
    parsnip, pumpkin, red/green/yellow capsicums)
2–3 tablespoons olive oil
1–2 cloves garlic, crushed, peeled and chopped
3–4 sprigs fresh thyme and/or rosemary (optional)

Preheat the oven to 200°C. Rinse the chicken inside (remove giblets etc.) and out and pat dry. Stab the lemon/s about six times with a sharp knife and place inside the chicken along with the garlic and fresh herbs.

Place chicken, breast side up, in a large roasting bag and add the olive oil. Massage the bag so the whole chicken has been coated with the oil, then tie the bag, leaving a finger-sized whole at the opening so steam can escape. Place the bag in a large roasting pan and put into the heated oven to begin to cook while you prepare the vegetables. The chicken will take 1¼–1½ hours, depending on size, to cook at 200°C.

Scrub (or peel, if you prefer) the root vegetables, then halve or quarter lengthwise depending on their size. Cut the pumpkin into wedges 4–5cm wide and deseed and quarter the capsicums. Put the vegetables in a large (unpunctured!) plastic bag, add the oil and crushed garlic and toss to coat all the vegetables with oil. Remove the vegetables from the bag and arrange in the pan with the herbs around the bagged chicken (add the capsicums 20–30 minutes after the other vegetables).

When the chicken has cooked for about 1¼–1½ hours, carefully remove it from the oven. (If the vegetables have not browned, place them under the grill for a few minutes.) Snip the corner from the oven bag and collect any juices to make gravy (see below). Slit the bag open with a sharp knife and check that the chicken is properly cooked (pierce the thickest part of the thigh with a sharp knife – if the juices run clear, not pink, the chicken is cooked).

Carve or break up the chicken and arrange the meat and vegetables on a warmed platter or serving plates.

Gravy

2 tablespoons flour
2 tablespoons olive oil
1–1½ cups chicken juices, stock, water or white wine
salt and pepper to taste

Measure the flour and olive oil into a non-stick frypan and mix to a smooth paste. Cook over a high heat until the mixture begins to colour, then gradually add the liquid and heat, stirring continuously to prevent lumps forming, until gravy boils and thickens. Season to taste with salt and pepper, then serve.

Eggplant stacks

These tasty stacks are a different and delicious way to use eggplant. The quantities given here will serve two adults, but it is very easy to multiply the quantities for larger numbers.

For 2 servings:

1 medium (about 300g) eggplant
2–3 tablespoons olive oil
salt and pepper
2–3 tablespoons chopped fresh basil (or 2 tablespoons
    basil pesto)
2–3 medium tomatoes, thinly sliced
6–8 black olives, chopped (optional)
1 cup grated or 100g thinly sliced mozzarella cheese

Turn the oven on to preheat to 200°C. Cut the eggplant lengthwise into 6 even slices. Lay these on a baking tray, and drizzle lightly with olive oil, then turn them over and do the same to the other side. Sprinkle lightly with salt and pepper, then bake for 12–15 minutes, until soft and beginning to brown.

Sprinkle each of the slices with some of the chopped basil (or brush with pesto) then cover the 4 larger slices of eggplant with sliced tomato. Sprinkle each with the chopped olives (if using), then sprinkle with grated cheese or cover with a thin layer of sliced cheese. Season with additional salt and pepper.

Re-assemble the eggplant halves by stacking the slices, more or less as they were cut. Sprinkle each half with any remaining cheese then bake at 200°C for another 10–12 minutes until the cheese has melted and the tomato has softened.

Serve immediately with a green salad and crusty bread.

Lemon-garlic-herb roasted chicken

Roast lamb with white beans and pesto

There's always something special about a roast leg of lamb, and I think this variation on the theme is extra special as well as a little out of the ordinary.

For 4–6 servings:

1 small-medium leg of lamb (1–1.5 kg)
2 cloves garlic, crushed, peeled and chopped
a few sprigs fresh thyme and rosemary
1 tablespoon olive oil
salt and pepper
3–4 cloves garlic, peeled
2 small-medium onions, quartered
2–3 medium capsicums (red, green or yellow), deseeded and quartered
400g can whole peeled tomatoes
3 x 300g cans butter beans
300g can tomato purée
½ cup red wine
1 teaspoon each dried basil and thyme
¼ – ½ cup additional wine or water if required
½ –1 teaspoon salt
black pepper to taste
extra fresh herbs to garnish

Turn the oven on to preheat to 180°C. Place the lamb leg on a board, trim off any excess fat, and make a dozen deep incisions over the surface. Stuff a little of the chopped garlic and fresh herbs into each hole. Rub all over with any remaining crushed garlic and the olive oil.

Place the lamb in a large, shallow casserole or roasting dish (about 20 x 35cm) and sprinkle with salt and pepper. Add the garlic cloves, onions and capsicums to the tray then place in the oven at 180°C.

Drain the can of tomatoes (reserving the juice), then crush and mix together with the beans, tomato purée, wine and herbs. When the lamb has cooked for 45–60 minutes, drain off any excess fat, then stir the bean mixture into the tray. Return the lamb to the oven and continue to cook, stirring the bean mixture once or twice, for a further 45–60 minutes (a smaller leg will take 1½ hours in total and a larger one about 2 hours). If the bean mixture begins to look dry, add the tomato juice, extra wine or water.

Remove from the oven and season the sauce to taste with salt and pepper. Arrange on a serving dish or on plates, garnished with some extra sprigs of fresh herbs. Serve accompanied with a large bowl of pesto (see below), some seasonal vegetables and crusty bread.

Pesto

For 1½ – 2 cups pesto:

4 cloves garlic, peeled
4 cups (about 150g) fresh basil, large stems removed
½ cup pine nuts
½ cup grated parmesan
½ –1 cup olive oil
salt to taste

Put the peeled garlic, basil leaves and pine nuts in a food processor and process until well chopped. Add the grated parmesan and ½ cup of olive oil and process again until well mixed. Start adding the extra olive oil a tablespoon at a time until you have a fairly smooth paste that just holds its shape.

Add salt to taste then transfer to airtight containers for storage. Pour a little extra oil on top of each container to help prevent browning.

Roast lamb with white beans and pesto

Sinfully rich chocolate cake

This cake is a chocoholic's dream! The quantities of chocolate and butter may sound excessive, but the result is so rich that a small serving tends to go a long way – I think it makes a good occasional treat.

For 8–10 servings:
1 cup strong coffee (instant or brewed)
300g semisweet chocolate bits or morsels
250g butter
1 tablespoon vanilla essence
2 tablespoons orange liqueur (or the grated rind of ½ an orange)
6 large eggs

Preheat the oven to 170°C (or 160°C if using a fan oven), and line the bottom of a 30cm springform tin with baking paper (or a teflon liner) and non-stick spray the sides.

Place the coffee and chocolate in a large microwave bowl and heat at 50% power, stirring at 1 minute intervals, until the chocolate has melted (if you use boiling coffee this should only take 1–2 minutes).

Cut the butter into cubes and add to the chocolate mixture. Stir occasionally until the butter has melted (warm again if necessary). Measure in the vanilla, orange liqueur (or rind) then add the eggs. Whisk until smooth, then pour the mixture into the prepared tin.

Bake for 25–30 minutes until just set in the middle, then remove from the oven – don't worry if the cake puffs and rises in large bubbles, these should settle again as it cools. Let the cake cool to room temperature, then refrigerate until firm (at least 2–3 hours). Run a knife around the edge, and then remove from the tin.

Dust with icing sugar or cocoa powder and serve in thin wedges.

Sinfully rich chocolate cake

Apricot cheesecake tartlets

These scrumptious little tartlets can be served for dessert, or anytime with tea or coffee. Making your own pastry may seem like a lot of trouble, but if you have a food processor it is really very simple (you don't even need to wash it between making the pastry and the filling).

For 16 tartlets:
Pastry
1 cup self-raising flour
75g cold butter, cubed
½ cup cottage cheese

Filling
¼ cup cottage cheese
¼ cup crème fraîche (or cream cheese)
1 medium egg
a few drops each almond and vanilla essence
about ¼ cup apricot jam

Preheat the oven to 180°C. Measure the flour into a food processor fitted with a metal chopping blade. Drop in the butter and process until it is cut through the flour. Measure in the cottage cheese and process again until evenly mixed. Check the dough – the mixture should resemble crumbs, but they should stick together to form a pliable dough when squeezed. If the mixture is too dry, add water a teaspoonful at a time, testing between each addition.

Tip the pastry mixture from the food processor and press together to form a ball. Place this in a plastic bag and refrigerate while you prepare the filling.

Place the second measure of cottage cheese in the food processor and process for about 30 seconds. Add the crème fraîche (or cream cheese), egg and essences and process until smooth and creamy.

Remove the dough from the fridge and, working on a lightly floured surface, roll it out to about 30–35cm square. Cut the sheet into 16 smaller (about 8 x 8cm) squares.

Non-stick spray 16 patty (or muffin) pans and gently press one of the small pastry squares into each. Fill each with ½–1 teaspoon of apricot jam then about a tablespoon of the custard filling mixture.

Bake the tartlets for 15–20 minutes, or until golden brown. Remove from the oven, then brush with warmed apricot jam to glaze.

Serve warm or cool for dessert or with tea or coffee.

Feijoa cream pie

If you like feijoas but are not sure how to cook them, simply replace the apples in your favourite apple pies and puddings with a similar quantity of sliced or chopped feijoas. Of course the flavour is different, since feijoas are perfumed and aromatic, but the results are delectable.

In this recipe the slightly grainy feijoas are complemented by a smooth creamy custard, in a flaky filo pastry crust, producing an elegant but easily prepared pie.

For 4–6 servings:
½ cup sugar
½ cup sour cream
1 teaspoon vanilla essence
½ teaspoon cinnamon
3 large eggs
5–6 (350g) large feijoas
3 tablespoons butter
6 sheets filo pastry

Preheat the oven to 180°C. Measure the sugar, sour cream, vanilla and cinnamon into a blender or food processor. Add the eggs and blend or process until smooth and creamy.

Top and tail, then peel the feijoas, then cut each (crosswise) into 3–4 slices about 2 cm thick. (Don't do this too far in advance or the feijoas will brown.)

Melt the butter and non-stick spray a 22–25cm pie plate. Lay the first sheet of filo across the pie dish, then lightly press it down, leaving the excess at the ends protruding. Brush lightly with some of the melted butter, then turn the dish a little and add the next sheet with its ends protruding at a slightly different angle. Repeat this process until all the filo sheets have been used.

Arrange the feijoa slices in a single layer over the bottom of the dish, then pour in the egg mixture. Fold and arrange the protruding filo corners at interesting angles. Place the pie in the oven and bake at 180°C for 30–35 minutes, or until the pastry is golden brown and the custard filling has set.

Remove from the oven and dust lightly with icing sugar just before serving.

Note:
This pie can be served hot, warm or cold, but really looks at its best within 30 minutes of baking (after this time the fruit tends to shrink away from the custard).

Fruity dessert cake

This delicious 'mix in the pot' cake makes a great dessert any time of year. You can make it with one or two seasonal (or canned) fruits and the nuts of your choice!

For 6–8 servings:
¼ cup chopped walnuts, toasted almonds or toasted
    hazelnuts
1 tablespoon sugar
150g butter
1 cup sugar
2 large eggs
1 teaspoon vanilla
1½ cups self-raising flour
1 teaspoon baking powder
1–2 cups ripe, cubed/sliced raw fruit*
½ cup berries (optional)

Preheat the oven to 180°C. Toast the nuts lightly under a grill or in the oven as it preheats. Chop toasted nuts finely, mix with the first measure of sugar and put aside.

Melt the butter in a microwave bowl or pot until just liquid. Add the second measure of sugar, the eggs, and vanilla and beat until blended. Sift the flour and baking powder into the bowl, then add half the nut and sugar mixture and mix gently.

Spread mixture evenly into a lightly oiled or non-stick sprayed 23–25cm round (preferably loose bottomed) cake tin. Prepare the fruit, cutting it into 2cm chunks, or slicing. Arrange pieces, skin side up, in the batter. Sprinkle the top with berries (if using) then with the remaining sugar-nut mixture.

Bake at 180°C for about 45 minutes, until cake mixture has risen round the fruit and browned lightly, and the centre springs back when pressed. Remove from the oven and cool on a rack.

Dust with icing sugar, cut into wedges, and serve warm. A dollop of lightly whipped cream or natural yoghurt make good accompaniments.

*Suitable fruits include peaches, nectarines, plums, strawberries, raspberries, blueberries and blackberries. Drained canned fruit pieces also work well.

Sour cream lemon tart

This simple tart makes an impressive finale to any meal!

For a 20cm tart (6–8 servings):
250g sweet short pastry (1 sheet pre-rolled)
½ cup sugar
thinly peeled or grated rind of ½ lemon (see below)
2 tablespoons lemon juice
2 teaspoons custard powder (or cornflour)
1 cup (250g) sour cream
3 large eggs

Preheat the oven to 150°C. While the oven heats, non-stick spray (or butter) a 20cm pie or flan dish (preferably with a removable base and fluted sides). Gently press the sheet of pastry into the pan and trim off any excess.

Measure the sugar into a food processor. Using a potato peeler, thinly peel the yellow rind from the lemon, or grate it finely – vary the quantity according to taste. Add the rind to the sugar, then process until the rind is cut finely through the sugar.

Mix the lemon juice with the custard powder (or cornflour). Add the sour cream and the lemon juice mixture to the sugar, then process until smooth and the sugar has dissolved. Add the eggs one at a time with the processor running.

Pour the filling mixture into the pastry base, then bake for 40–50 minutes, or until the top is beginning to brown around the edges (the middle may still jiggle a little, but this is OK).

Remove tart from the oven, allow to cool (the middle will probably sink a little and become firmer).

Serve cut into wedges, topped with a spoonful of crème fraîche or lightly whipped cream and sprinkled with a curl or a few grated strands of lemon rind.

Double chocolate and hazelnut brownies

Everyone seems to love brownies! For something so simple to make they are quite versatile – serve them warm from the oven with vanilla ice cream for dessert, cool and cut into fingers to put in lunches or to serve with coffee.

For a 23cm square pan:
½ cup canola oil
125g white chocolate, chopped
1 cup brown sugar
1 teaspoon vanilla essence
2 large eggs
1 cup flour
½ teaspoon baking powder
½ teaspoon salt
½ – ¾ cup lightly roasted hazelnuts, roughly chopped
½ cup (90g) dark chocolate bits

Turn the oven on to 180°C (or 170°C for a fan oven), and thoroughly non-stick spray and/or line a 23cm square tin with baking paper or a teflon liner.

Combine the oil and white chocolate in a medium-sized pot or microwave bowl. Heat gently, stirring frequently, until the chocolate has melted. Remove from the heat and cool for 5 minutes, then add the sugar, vanilla and eggs and stir until the mixture is smooth.

Sift in the flour, baking powder and salt, and stir gently until evenly mixed. Add the chopped nuts and dark chocolate bits, and stir until just combined (if the mixture is too warm the dark chocolate bits will melt and 'marble' the mixture).

Pour the mixture into the tin and bake for 25–30 minutes, or until a skewer poked into the centre comes out clean. Cool, then remove from the tin and cut into squares or fingers.

Variation:
Replace hazelnuts with almonds, pecans or macadamia nuts.

Carrot and pineapple muffins

These muffins are based on the familiar carrot cake, however, like most muffins, they are very quick and much easier to make than cakes – there is no beating or creaming of butter and sugar involved.

Try them served after dinner with tea or coffee, or enjoy them any time of the day. If you want to dress them up, why not ice them with cream cheese icing when they are cool?

For 12 medium muffins:
2 cups wholemeal flour
4 teaspoons baking powder
¾ cup brown sugar
2 teaspoons cinnamon
1 teaspoon mixed spice
½ –1 teaspoon salt
½ cup chopped walnuts
1 cup (150g) grated carrot
227g can crushed pineapple
¼ cup orange juice
1 large egg
¼ cup canola oil (or 50g butter, melted)

Preheat the oven to 200°C, then measure the first seven ingredients into a large bowl. Use the larger amount of salt if you are using oil rather than butter. Mix well using your hands, making sure that there are no large lumps of sugar in the mixture.

Grate the carrot. If you are not sure of the quantity, weigh the carrot before grating it, or pack the grated carrot firmly into a cup measure. Mix the grated carrot, the pineapple in its juice, the orange juice and egg together in another bowl. Stir in the oil or melted butter, then add this liquid to the flour mixture.

Fold everything together, until the flour is just moistened. Take care to avoid over-mixing, as this will toughen the muffins. Add a little extra orange juice if the mixture is too thick to drop from the spoon.

Spoon the mixture into 12 non-stick sprayed or lightly oiled medium (regular) muffin pans. Bake at 200°C for 12–15 minutes, or until the muffins spring back when pressed in the middle. Remove muffin tray/s from the oven and leave to cool for 3–4 minutes before tipping muffins from the pans and cooling on a rack.

Variation:
Cool muffins on rack then ice with cream cheese icing made by mixing together 1½ cups icing sugar, 2–3 tablespoons cream cheese and 1–2 tablespoons lemon juice.

Sticky date puddings

I think there is something particularly nice about being served your own little pudding for dessert. I borrowed the idea for these from a friend's mother – she keeps a supply of them in her freezer, to produce when required. While the puddings thaw in the microwave, she prepares the sauce.

For 6 individual (or one 23cm square) pudding/s:
1 cup (about 175g) pitted dates, chopped
1 cup hot water
50g butter
1 cup self-raising flour
½ teaspoon baking soda
1 teaspoon cinnamon
½ teaspoon mixed spice
¾ cup lightly packed brown sugar
2 large eggs

Place the roughly chopped dates in a medium-sized microwave bowl. Cover with the water then microwave on high power (100%) for 5 minutes, stirring occasionally. Stir in the butter, then set aside to cool.

Sift the flour, baking soda and spices into another medium bowl, then stir in the brown sugar. Add the eggs to the date mixture, stir until well combined, then fold this into the dry ingredients.

Divide the mixture between 6 large non-stick sprayed or oiled muffin pans, or pour into a prepared 23cm cake tin. Cover muffin tins with foil, then place in a roasting pan containing 2cm of boiling water. Bake at 180°C (or 170°C fan-bake) for 25–30 minutes, until puddings are firm when pressed in the centres. Leave to stand for 5 minutes before removing from pans. (Bake the large pudding uncovered for 30 minutes or until centre is firm when pressed.)

Serve warm topped with the sauce below.

Butterscotch Sauce

1 cup sour cream
1 cup brown sugar
2 tablespoons orange liqueur or grated rind
    of ½ an orange

Combine all ingredients and heat until sugar dissolves. (For a thicker sauce, simmer, stirring frequently, for 5–10 minutes.)

Note:

Each large muffin tin holds about 1 cup of mixture. Use other containers if preferred.

Lemon-lime cheesecake

A rich, moist 'traditional-style' baked cheesecake, with a citrus twist – ideal for special occasions!

For a 20cm cheesecake (8–10 servings):
250g packet digestive biscuits
100g butter, melted
3 x 250g cartons cream cheese
¾ cup sugar
finely grated rind of 1 lemon and 1 lime
3 tablespoons lemon and/or lime juice
3 large eggs

Crush or food-process the biscuits into fine crumbs (if you don't have a food processor, place the biscuits in a plastic bag and bang with a rolling pin).

Melt the butter then mix it evenly through the biscuit crumbs. Non-stick spray (or butter) a 20–23cm springform cake tin, then press the crumb mixture into the base and up the sides of the tin, trying to get an even thickness.

Beat or process together the cream cheese, sugar, finely grated lemon and lime rind and juice until the mixture is light and fluffy. Add the eggs and process until evenly mixed.

Carefully pour the cream cheese mixture into the prepared base, and bake at 150°C for about 1 hour, or until the centre is just firm. Cool, then refrigerate until ready to serve.

Cut into wedges and top with lightly whipped cream or yoghurt and passionfruit pulp to serve.

weights & measures

As most cooks do not have scales in their kitchen, where possible measurements are indicated in cups and tablespoons. Small quantities of butter are measured in tablespoons, and larger quantities are given by weight.

In New Zealand, South Africa, the USA and in England, 1 tablespoon equals 15ml. In Australia, 1 tablespoon equals 20ml. These variations will not adversely affect the end result, as long as the same spoon is used consistently, so the proportions are correct.

Grams to Ounces and vice versa

General	Exact
30g = 1oz	1oz = 28.35g
60g = 2oz	2oz = 56.70g
90g = 3oz	3oz = 85.05g
120g = 4oz	4oz = 113.04g
150g = 5oz	5oz = 141.08g
180g = 6oz	6oz = 170.01g
210g = 7oz	7oz = 198.04g
230g = 8oz	8oz = 226.08g
260g = 9oz	9oz = 255.01g
290g = 10oz	10oz = 283.05g
320g = 11oz	11oz = 311.08g
350g = 12oz	12oz = 340.02g
380g = 13oz	13oz = 368.05g
410g = 14oz	14oz = 396.09g
440g = 15oz	15oz = 425.02g
470g = 16oz	16oz = 453.06g

Recipes based on these (International Units) rounded values

Liquid Measurements

25ml   (28.4ml) =1 fl oz
150ml   (142ml) = 5 fl oz = ¼ pint = 1 gill
275ml   (284ml) =10 fl oz = ½ pint
425ml   (426ml) =15 fl oz = ¾ pint
575ml   (568ml) =20 fl oz = 1 pint

Spoon Measures

¼ teaspoon = 1.25ml
½ teaspoon = 2.5ml
1 teaspoon   = 5ml
1 tablespoon = 15ml
In NZ, SA, USA and UK 1 tablespoon = 15ml
In Australia 1 tablespoon = 20ml

Measurements

cm to approx inches

0.5cm = ¼"		5cm = 2"	
1.25cm = ½"		7.5cm = 3"	
2.5cm = 1"		10cm = 4"	

Cake Tin Sizes

cm to approx inches

15cm = 6"	23cm = 9"
18cm = 7"	25cm = 10"
20cm = 8"	

Oven Temperatures

Celsius to Farenheit

110°C	225°F – very cool
130°C	250°F
140°C	275°F – cool
150°C	300°F
170°C	325°F – warm
180°C	350°F – moderate
190°C	375°F – fairly hot
200°C	400°F
220°C	425°F – hot
230°C	450°F – very hot
240°C	475°F

Abbreviations

g	grams
kg	kilogram
mm	millimetre
cm	centimetre
ml	millilitre
°C	degrees celsius

American-Imperial

in.	inch
lb.	pound
oz.	ounce